Life Beyond the Altar pt. 1

HOW TO LOVE GOD BACK

Written by Erik K. Nance
For
The University of Believers

Nevertheless I have somewhat against thee, because thou hast left

thy first love – Jesus in Revelations 2:5

Table of Contents

- You've said YES! 11
- The Love Language of God 15
- Understanding Grace.. 56
- The 4 Keys to Unlocking Love............................ 83
- John 3:16 Revealed... 100
- Behold The Lamb of God.................................... 110
- Would You Still Say YES?................................... 120

PRAYER

Dear heavenly Father,

My heart is drawn to you. My soul craves you and your presence. I know you love me, reveal unto me the ways you want me to love you back. I surrender all to the God that gave me all, YOU! I pray my heart is not hardened, but the Holy Spirit lead and guide me into all truth.

In the name of your dear son Jesus, amen!

You've Said YES!

*D*id your soul not cry out for more? Did your heart not yearn for a relationship with the King of kings and Lord of lords? Did the angels not rejoice when you said, "Yes" to Christ? Paul says, in Romans 10:19, that if we believe in our heart and confess with our mouth that God raised Jesus from the dead, then we <u>shall be</u> saved! You said yes to God, and even though you may have been on the edge of your bed or in a church filled with others, in the spirit you were at an altar of marriage and a new life has begun in you!

Marriage between man and woman is an earthly interpretation of a relationship between God and man. After the wedding, the honeymoon stage occurs. No problems, just "I love you, I love you!" and "even though you look like this in the morning, I still love you!" The only reason the honeymoon stage ends is because one of the two parties fails to TRUST, fails to COMMUNICATE, fails to SUBMIT and eventually they lose hope in the VISION they've once shared.

In many cases the two parties tend to bring old problems, old lifestyles, and ancient concepts into a covenant that is supposed to be brand new. For most of our lives it's been all about us, so we tend to bring a "ME" mindset into a marriage that can only survive with a unified attitude of "WE". Because of the "ME" mindset, many of our spiritual marriages that began so full of bliss and so full of God are now dying, choking and in desperate need of LOVE.

Consider what happened to satan when he was disbarred from the highest heaven, it was no longer about making God's vision work, it was about satan implementing *his* vision in a relationship that could not accommodate it. Satan usurped the authority of God for the authority of "ME", and that mindset does not work well with the God we serve.

Also, consider Adam and Eve. They lived the life that we all want. They had good jobs, God was with them daily, and everlasting life was continuously in the midst of them. Now think about the Tree of Knowledge of Good and Evil; what was so wrong about knowing good and evil? Why would God change His entire plan for man due to the tree of knowledge of good and evil? Understand this - God's good and evil already existed. The commandment was given: be fruitful and multiply, keep and subdue the land and STAY AWAY FROM SATAN! That was God's good, and breaking it, well, that was God's evil. When you look at the two words -good and evil- in their original Hebrew form, you see that the definitions deal distinctly with the sensual and intellectual states of man. How do *I FEEL* things should go? What do *I THINK* about what God said? Once knowledge of self, squares off with every word that proceeds out of the mouth of God, sin occurs.

Therefore, marriage with you and God is an act of surrendering, not God surrendering to you, but you surrendering unto God. We must go from "what I think" to what He said. Jesus says we should live by "EVERY WORD" that proceeds out of the mouth of God. Really think about that for a second. Jesus says we should be governed by the words of God; the things He wrote, not by the things we feel should frame our world.

What stage are you in your relationship with Christ? Have you confessed with your mouth, believed in your heart, and then brought God into a house filled with old bags that you won't let go of? Have you been walking on cloud nine, without considering your better half, which is God? What does He require of you? What does He desire of you? Have you read His 66 love letters He left for you? Do you have the attitude of "Give me! I want! This is what I THINK! This is how I FEEL!" or have you left room for God's will to be accomplished in your life? These are real questions that we as Christians should ask ourselves daily!

Millions of Israelites wandered in the wilderness because they didn't consider their better half. They said "yes" with their mouths but their mindset and movement towards submission to God said "no". Therefore the bible refers to those Israelites as non-believers! Faith + Action = A true believer in Christ, not just faith alone.

Don't live another day under your own authority. It killed a lot of "so-called believers" then, and it's killing a lot of "so-called believers" now. Yahweh says in Isaiah that His ways are higher than our ways, and His thoughts are higher than our thoughts. In Proverbs, Solomon tells us not to lean towards our own understanding but in all thy ways acknowledge Him. Jesus says, "Pick up your cross and follow me." Christ is not our co-pilot. This God wants it all! Follow HIM, for only He knows how to take you far beyond the honeymoon stage and usher you into a place called eternity.

See you in the next chapter...

The Love Language of God

1 John 4:19 says:

We love him, because He first loved us.

God's love is so amazing, so vast, so incredible and extremely comforting. John is saying, that because of His love being so good, it should drive us to love Him back. When I look back, I remember the many times I didn't see any way out and how He created a path for me. When life seemed so dark, He became light for me. When there was absolutely no way, He became my way, and that was all because He loved me. Then one day I was faced with a question within, as I asked myself, do I really love God back? I mean, for a God that does so much and loves so hard, I had to ask myself, am I doing my part in this relationship? Once I studied His word, the results were shocking! The Word clearly showed me that not only did I <u>not</u> love God back, but I was also headed to The Lake of Fire because I didn't.

My quest started with a question, "If God so loved the world according to John 3:16, then why does the bible say that most of the world wouldn't get into His kingdom?" At the end of my multi year quest, it was evident; the Kingdom of God will be filled with people who loved God back!

The foundation for just about every topic in The Word of God is found in the first five books of the bible. Want to know what evil is or how to become righteous - the first five books of the bible. Want to know how to get blessed, or why people are cursed - the first five books of the bible. Want to understand Paul, Peter, James and Jesus better - first five books of the bible. Therefore when it comes to the most important feat God requires of man, which is to love Him back, we must start in the first five books as well.

Let's start our journey in Exodus the 20th chapter. This is the first time we see a compiled list of the 10 commandments all in one place. It's also the first time we see God making mention of loving Him back. Let's investigate!

Exodus 20:5-6:

Thou shalt not bow down thyself to them, nor serve them (*speaking of other gods*): for I the Lord thy God am a jealous God, visiting the iniquity of the fathers upon the children unto the third and fourth generation of them that <u>hate me</u>; and showing mercy unto thousands of them that <u>love me</u>, and <u>keep my commandments</u>.

If this were the only scripture in the bible that talked about loving God, which its not, I would gather two major things;

    1) Loving God and keeping His commandments are

synonymous with one another

2) Knowingly or not, there are a people who hate Him, and those are one's who don't obey the commandments of God

With knowledge of Jesus' words in Revelations 3, which we'll touch on later, He says to the Lukewarm He would "spue" them from His mouth, the world seems to lie in only two categories:

1) Those that Love Him
2) Those that Hate Him

This is validated by the parables Jesus speaks as He separates the world into two groups; the sheep vs. the goats, the wheat vs. the tares, the line in which we stand will indicate entrance into Eternal Life or Eternal Damnation.

Let's continue to investigate!

In the book of Deuteronomy, Moses reiterates the 10 commandments along with statutes and decrees that hang off of them, and then in Chapter 6 we see a very familiar phrase for the first time.

Deuteronomy 6:4-5:

Hear, O Israel: The Lord our God is one Lord: And thou shalt love the Lord thy God with all thine heart, and with all thy soul, and with all thy might.

For the first time in the bible we see that God commands us to Love Him with all our heart, our entire mind and all our soul. Basically, God is requiring us to love Him with all we've got! While reading this scripture, a question arose in my heart.

How?

How do you want us to love you? In marriage I realized everyone has a love language; what's God's? I've read You want me to love You with all I've got, but what does that mean? I don't want my 'with all I've got' be completely opposite of 'what you require'! There's no question about it, we must find out what loving God with all our heart, mind and soul means to <u>Him</u>, the only person that matters.

The next verse gives us some leeway in our quest.

Deuteronomy 6:6:

And these words, which I command thee this day, shall be in thine heart.

Moses tells the people that the words he told them that day, which if we look to chapter five we'll see it was the 10 commandments, should be inside of us. It seems as if Moses is making a correlation between the two. Maybe, just maybe, Moses is saying that loving God

18

with all we've got has something to do with obeying His commandments. Let's continue to investigate!

Deuteronomy 7:9-11:

> Know therefore that the Lord thy God, he is God, the faithful
> God, which keepeth covenant and mercy with them that love
> him and keep his commandments to a thousand generations;
> And repayeth them that hate him to their face, to destroy
> them: he will not be slack to him that hateth him, he will repay
> him to his face. Thou shalt therefore keep the commandments,
> and the statutes, and the judgments, which I command thee
> this day, to do them.

This is wonderful and scary at the same time! The wonderful part is that God says He keeps covenant and mercy with the people that love Him. Can you imagine, every covenant that God has created with Abraham, Isaac and Jacob being yours? There is not one covenant for anyone else that isn't an Israelite. Therefore Paul lets us know in Romans 2:29 that the Jew, in God's eyes, isn't one who is born a Jew, but is one inwardly. Once we accept the <u>adoption</u> into His spiritual family, and Love Him back, God's covenant of peace, protection, eternal life and blessings are now all of ours. It's not just for those that walk around and say Abraham's blessings are mine; it's for those that Love God back. Then there's the scary part; God brings up these people that hate Him again. For the second time we see those that hate him would

19

eventually not obey the commandments Moses gave them that day, which were again the 10 commandments and the statutes and decrees that hang off of them. We also notice that loving God and keeping His commandments go hand in hand with each other. As a matter of fact, Moses tells them to love God, and then in verse 11 says <u>therefore obey</u> His commandments.

It seems pretty clear based upon the first five books of the bible that loving God and obedience towards His commandments are on one accord with one another. But what about the rest of the bible? Do they paint another picture? Lets investigate this so we can have a clear, holistic picture painted on the subject of Loving God.

Nehemiah 1:5:

And said, I beseech thee, O LORD God of heaven, the great and terrible God, that keepeth covenant and mercy for them that love him and observe his commandments.

Again, Nehemiah acknowledges the correlation between loving Him and keeping His commandments.

2nd Kings 23:25:

And like unto him was there no king before him, that turned to the LORD with all his heart, and with all his soul, and with all his might, according to all the law of Moses; neither after him arose there any like him.

This passage is about King Josiah. The bible says that Josiah loved God back by obeying all the commandments that Moses had written. So even post Moses, pre Christ, we see obeying God's commandments lead to loving God with all we had. But what about the New Testament, did Jesus change the system we've grown accustomed too reading?

Lets delve into the words of Jesus!

Matthew 22:37-40:

Jesus said unto him, Thou shalt love the Lord thy God with all thy heart, and with all thy soul, and with all thy mind. This is the first and great commandment. And the second is like unto it, Thou shalt love thy neighbour as thyself. On these two commandments hang all the law and the prophets.

Christ says that on those two requirements, hang the other commandments written in the first five books of the bible as well as the words spoken by His prophets. This lines up with everything we've read thus far. Jesus is telling us that loving God with all we've got is the first commandment along with loving others as ourselves. We've covered the loving God part, but what about loving thy neighbor? Does that speak to the 10 commandments, the decrees and statutes that hang off of them as well? Lets quickly investigate this!

Leviticus the 19th chapter deals with how God wants us to deal with our neighbors. He covers the last 6 of the 10 commandments such as stealing, lying etc. Let's see how God instructed Moses to sum these things up.

Leviticus 19:18:

But thou shalt love thy neighbour as thyself: I am the Lord.

Paul received the same revelation as he speaks about this in Romans 13:9:

For this, Thou shalt not commit adultery, Thou shalt not kill, Thou shalt not steal, Thou shalt not bear false witness, Thou shalt not covet; and if there be any other commandment, it is briefly comprehended in this saying, namely, Thou shalt love thy neighbour as thyself.

We see that what Jesus says's lines up to what God told Moses. We also see that Loving God and your neighbor are direct attachments to obeying the 10 commandments, statutes and decrees that hang off of them. As a matter of fact, Jesus gets very direct, hours before His death.

John 14:15 Jesus says:

If you love me, keep my commandments.

John 14:21 Jesus says:

He that hath my commandments, and keepeth them, he it is

that loveth me: and he that loveth me shall be loved of my Father, and I will love him, and will manifest myself to him.

John 14:23 Jesus says:

If a man love me, he will keep my words:

John 15:14:

Ye are my friends, if ye do whatsoever I command you.

Jesus' disciples forsook all they had to follow Him. He was their friend, their pastor, their leader, their teacher, as well as their brother. They loved Him according to their emotions; however, Christ felt a need to remind them that IF you want to love me, do what I've asked you to do. And even though they'd been with Him the past three and a half years, there was no other way for Him to manifest Himself, nor the Father to fall in love with them if they didn't!

Often I've heard teacher's say, "Jesus said MY commandments, and Jesus' commandments are, love the Lord with all you heart mind and soul and your neighbor as yourself." Well, since we now understand that Christ was referring to the 10 commandments and things that hang off of them, questions arose:

Are the 10 commandments along with the statutes and decrees Jesus' words?

When did Jesus' words start?

Did they begin in Matthew or did they begin in Genesis?

These are very important questions. Are Jesus' words simply the words in red or are they the words Moses spoke as well. We've found that Loving God equates to keeping those commandments handed down by Moses, but were those words Moses' or Jesus'? Lets investigate!

In the book of Revelations Jesus begins speaking through His angel to John some say 60 years after His resurrection. He instructed John to write everything down and send it to His churches, which He knew would eventually reach us. Listen to what Jesus says concerning Himself:

1. Revelation 1:8 - I am Alpha and Omega, the beginning and the ending, saith the Lord, which is, and which was, and which is to come, the Almighty.
2. Revelation 1:11 - Saying, I am Alpha and Omega, the first and the last.
3. Revelation 21:6 - And he said unto me, It is done. I am Alpha and Omega, the beginning and the end.
4. Revelation 22:13 - I am Alpha and Omega, the beginning and the end, the first and the last.

Four times Jesus lets us know that He is the first and the last; the same one in the beginning and the same one in the end. But does this line up to the rest of the bible? Is this true? Was He the one in the beginning? The one who gave Moses the 10 Commandments? The one who cut the covenants with our forefathers? The one who created the world and rested on the seventh day? Was He the God that dealt with man? Let's investigate!

John 1:1-3 tells us that "In the beginning was the Word, and the Word was with God, and the Word was God. The same was in the beginning with God. All things were made by him; and without him was not any thing made that was made." In verse 14 and throughout the book of John, it lets us know that the "WORD" is Jesus. Therefore if you substitute The Word with Jesus, it'll read like this.

John 1:1-3:

> In the beginning was JESUS, and JESUS was with God, and JESUS was God. The same was in the beginning with God. All things were made by JESUS; and without JESUS was not any thing made that was made.

So Jesus was in the beginning and he made all things. But what about men such as Moses and Abraham, did He deal with them as well?

John 5 & John 6 says this:

John 5:37:

> And the Father himself, which hath sent me, hath borne witness of me. Ye have neither heard his voice at <u>any time</u>, nor

seen his shape.

John 6:46:

> Not that <u>any man</u> hath seen the Father, save he which is of God, he hath seen the Father.

Christ was letting them know, that no one had seen nor heard from the Father until He showed up in the flesh. So who did the seventy elders sit and eat with in the Old Testament? Who spoke to the people at Mount Sinai? Who talked to Abraham, and Moses, and Isaiah and David? Who gave Moses the various laws? JESUS, aka Yahweh the Son.

Jesus says this in John 8:58:

> Your father Abraham rejoiced to <u>see my day</u>: and <u>he saw it</u>, and was glad. Then said the Jews unto him, Thou art not yet fifty years old, and hast thou seen Abraham? Jesus said unto them, Verily, verily, I say unto you, Before Abraham was, <u>I am</u>.

Jesus was, He is, and He is to come. Paul also spoke on this wise in 1 Corinthians 10:1-4:

> Moreover, brethren, I would not that ye should be ignorant, how that all our fathers were under the cloud, and all passed through the sea; And were all baptized unto Moses in the cloud and in the sea; And did all eat the same spiritual meat; And did all drink the same spiritual drink: for they drank of that

spiritual Rock that followed them: and that Rock was Christ.

Paul also gives credit to Jesus being the head of the Israelites during the forty years of wilderness in Hebrews the 4th chapter. All of His followers knew and understood that Christ didn't start with Mary, He simply came through Mary. Therefore when Jesus says "My Commandments" they start in Genesis, not Matthew. This also sheds light on what Christ says in John 12:46-48:

> I am come a light into the world, that whosoever believeth on me should not abide in darkness. And if any man hear my words, and believe not, I judge him not: for I came not to judge the world, but to save the world. He that rejecteth me, and receiveth not my words, hath one that judgeth him: the word that I have spoken, the same shall judge him in the last day.

We will be judged by those words. Not just the ones in red, but the ones beginning in Genesis 1:1! The same God, the same words! Deuteronomy 10:12-13 says that keeping His commandments, which coincides with loving God back, is what God requires of man. As a matter of fact, Jesus says this lifestyle also equals eternal life! Let's read it in Luke 10:25-27:

> And, behold, a certain lawyer stood up, and tempted him, saying, Master, what shall I do to inherit eternal life? Jesus said unto him, What is written in the law? how readest thou? And the lawyer answering said, Thou shalt love the Lord thy

God with all thy heart, and with all thy soul, and with all thy strength, and with all thy mind; and thy neighbour as thyself.

Follow this very closely. The man asked Christ how to get eternal life. Jesus replied to him, asking, how do you interpret the law? The law He's speaking of is the books of Moses, aka the first five books of the bible. The master in the law replied and said the exact things we've previously read, that Loving God with all your heart mind and soul and you neighbor as yourself, summarize the 10 commandments and that decrees and statutes that hang off of them. But what Jesus has to say in response to him is shocking!

Verse 28:

Jesus said unto him, Thou hast answered right: this do, and thou shalt live.

Get this, Jesus told that lawyer YOU ARE RIGHT, DO THIS, AND GET ETERNAL LIFE. Believe it or not, obedience really makes God happy. He's so loving; allowing the sun to come out each morning, supplies air for us to breathe and a moon to shine in darkness over the saint and the sinner. He puts out so much that we tend to forget that His commandments are here for our very own good, in this life and to usher us into the life to come.

After spending three and half years with Jesus, lets see what His disciples have to say concerning the matter:

2 John 1:6:

> And this is love, that we walk after his commandments. This is
> the commandment, That, as ye have heard from the beginning,
> ye should walk in it.

1 John 5:3:

> For this is the love of God, that we keep his commandments:
> and his commandments are not grievous.

Get this, John is saying "keeping His commandments is how you love God" then turns around and says their not hard to do. Boy was this a revelation for me. For I've been taught to think His commandments were to hard, but then I realized how easy it was to clean the car when it was a reward at the end. How easy it was to spend my last on a girl that I liked a lot. How non-relevant it use to be to walk miles to a friends home, just to see them. Loving is easy when your in love!

From what we've learned, obeying the commandments of God doesn't equal loving God, rather it's a bi-product of loving Him. They go hand in hand, like faith and works. Think about the rich young ruler. He kept the commandments but didn't love God enough to leave all that he had and follow Him. God wants a real relationship, full of communication, praise, alone time and other things that would make any real relationship work. He let the world know that if you chose to love me, then make sure you don't forget to keep my commandments. It's easy to forget to love Him back because He loves so hard. He may have given you a mate out of nowhere, or paid a bill, or blessed your mom. Sometimes we tend to think that His acts of kindness must mean our acts are sufficient and that's not the case. God will love you until the end, but in the end, if you don't love Him back, you'll miss it! Jesus expressed His frustration with not receiving the love He desired in Revelations the 3rd chapter. He says in verse 16:

"I know thy works, that thou art neither cold nor hot: I would thou wert cold or hot. So then because thou art lukewarm, and neither cold nor hot, I will spue thee out of my mouth."

Doesn't this sound like someone who is fed up and frustrated? God wants to be loved back, and scriptures such as these remind us how serious loving God back is. Too often we think that because God is love, He is not to be feared; this mindset couldn't be further from the truth. God's wrath is real. This is also the same God who will wipe away more than 1,000,000,000 off this earth during the great tribulation. The same God who burned Sodom and Gomorrah, the same God that ordered the deaths of thousands of His people, the Benjamites, for sin. This is also the God that killed the first born of every Egyptian during the time of Moses and the same God who killed Ananias and Sapphira for lying to Peter. God's wrath occurs when the necessity to love Him back becomes over looked.

Those were tough pills for me to swallow, but then I started to think about myself and the relationships that didn't work out in my own life. A break up always occurred when one of the two parties felt their feelings were over looked and taken advantage of. Before every break up warnings were given. "I'm not happy when you do this." "Don't cheat on me, or I'll leave you!" Either one of the two parties simply doesn't care or rather they don't believe that a real break up is on its way. This leads me to my next question:

Will God break up with you?

Think about it. Would God send Christians, who call upon His name, into the Lake of Fire? The answer is yes! His WORD is His book of warnings! God has another book called the Lambs Book of Life where all those that are His are named. But one thing we don't hear preached is that Jesus blots names out of it. Exodus 32:33 says;

And the LORD said to Moses, "Whoever has sinned against Me, I will blot him out of My book."

God wants us to be victorious in this lifetime. Our number one deterrent from the life of victory is sin. Sin is what takes one from righteous to unrighteous, good to evil, in the Lambs Book of Life to out of it.

There use to be a very simple equation that God created that went like this:

SIN = DEATH...period!

But now that Christ has died for our sins there is a new equation God has for us:

SIN + REPENTANCE = LIFE...period!

The merciful God we serve encourages us to leave a life of sin behind with an act called repentance. God says in Isaiah 55:7:

> Let the wicked forsake his way, and the unrighteous man his thoughts: and let him return unto the Lord, and he will have mercy upon him; and to our God, for he will abundantly pardon.

God forgives a sinner once they've repented, which means turns from his or her sins. So why is there so many scriptures dealing with God sending Christians to the lake of fire? Let's investigate!

Matthew 7:21-24:

> Not everyone who says to Me, 'Lord, Lord,' shall enter the kingdom of heaven, but he who does the will of My Father in heaven. Many will say to Me in that day, 'Lord, Lord, have we not prophesied in Your name, cast out demons in Your name, and done many wonders in Your name?' And then I will declare to them, 'I never knew you; depart from Me, you who practice lawlessness!

Let's point out some facts in this story;

o These people are His church

o They called upon the name of the Lord

o They Prophesied

o They casted out demons

o They did great works in the sight of man

o They still lived in Sin

o Christ said, depart from me, you who practice lawlessness, which is sin!

Can you imagine? The best prophets, the best healers, the best workers for God, going to the lake of fire because of non-repented sin? This is how important it is to love God back. When you love God, you will find out His ways, His commandments, His laws and then FOLLOW THEM. Look at the first thing Christ said in verse 21; It's not the people who call on Jesus; it's the people that call AND do what He told them to! When that doesn't happen, separation occurs.

Let's locate another!

We're about to read a parable of a wedding. The story is symbolic of God accepting the Gentiles and other Nations into His church. Once the person was accepted into His church and was being prepared to be at the wedding between The Lamb and New Jerusalem as outlined in Revelations 21, we see one member of His church gets kicked out.

Lets pick up the story from there...

Matthew 22:8-13:

Then saith he to his servants, The wedding is ready, but they which were bidden were not worthy. Go ye therefore into the highways, and as many as ye shall find, bid to the marriage. So those servants went out into the highways, and gathered together all as many as they found, both bad and good: and the wedding was furnished with guests. And when the king came in to see the guests, he saw there a man which had not on a wedding garment: And he saith unto him, Friend, how camest thou in hither not having a wedding garment? And he was speechless. Then said the king to the servants, Bind him hand and foot, and take him away, and cast him into outer darkness, there shall be weeping and gnashing of teeth.

I use to read this and say, "Boy I hope that's not me." Then God showed me how to be sure that it's not me.

The man got kicked out for the wrong garment. Will Christ come back looking for us to have on a garment? And if so, what is that garment suppose to look like? Let's investigate!

Revelation 16:15:

Behold, I come as a thief. Blessed is he that <u>watcheth, and keepeth his garments, lest he walk naked</u>, and they see his shame.

So, when Christ comes back HE IS looking for a garment before one enters into His wedding with New Jerusalem. But what is the garment He's looking for?

Revelations 3:4-5:

Thou hast a few names even in Sardis which have not defiled their garments; and they shall walk with me in white: for they are worthy. He that overcometh, the same shall be clothed in white raiment.

So we can see that the clothing is white, and those closed in this white raiment will have their name to remain in the book of life. But what is this an actual garment or a metaphor for something else?

Revelations 19:7-9:

Let us be glad and rejoice, and give honour to him: for the marriage of the Lamb is come, and his wife hath made herself ready. And to her was granted that she should be arrayed in fine linen, clean and white: for the fine linen is the righteousness of saints. And he saith unto me, Write, Blessed are they which are called unto the marriage supper of the Lamb. And he saith unto me, These are the true sayings of God.

So, the marriage will be accompanied by people in all white linen. The linen is a metaphor for RIGHTEOUSNESS. In other words, the people will be righteous!

Here's the million-dollar question; how can I become righteous. John tells us that those that do right are righteous. But are we to do right according to our minds, or His words? Let's investigate!

Deuteronomy 6:25:

And it shall be our righteousness, if we observe to do all these commandments before the LORD our God, as he hath commanded us.

(There is righteousness that has come outside of the law and we'll deal with UNDERSTAND law in the chapter Understanding Grace)

Everything points back to living by every word that proceeds out of the mouth of God. The righteous obey, and when they don't they repent and plead the blood and go back to a life of obedience.

Let's take a look at another example of the church He calls Pergamos. While reading this, understand two things;

1) This is Jesus' Church
2) We're Jesus' Church

Let's take a look, Revelations 3:12-17:

And to the angel of the church in Pergamos write; These things saith he which hath the sharp sword with two edges;

I know thy works, and where thou dwellest, even where Satan's seat is: and thou holdest fast my name, and hast not denied my faith, even in those days wherein Antipas was my faithful martyr, who was slain among you, where Satan dwelleth. But I have a few things against thee, because thou hast there them that hold the doctrine of Balaam, who taught Balac to cast a stumblingblock before the children of Israel, to eat things sacrificed unto idols, and to commit fornication. So hast thou also them that hold the doctrine of the Nicolaitanes, which thing I hate. Repent; or else I will come unto thee quickly, and will fight against them with the sword of my mouth. He that hath an ear, let him hear what the Spirit saith unto the churches; To him that overcometh will I give to eat of the hidden manna, and will give him a white stone, and in the stone a new name written, which no man knoweth saving he that receiveth it.

Let's follow closely what Jesus said:

- He knew their works
- They held fast to His name
- They had faith
- Someone died for His name

Now this is more than I can say for a lot of churches today. However notice the next few things that would shock the churches of our time:

- They had false doctrine, which means they hadn't cleaved to every word that proceeded out of God's mouth
- They ate the foods that were sacrificed to idols which God says is an abomination
- They committed fornication, either physically or spiritually against God and/or themselves

Now get this, Christ is still giving them the opportunity to repent. Even though they did some good and some bad, they were on their way to the lake of fire because of it. The little bit of bad will ruin an individual. Christ says, I will fight against you with the words of His mouth. That is the same thing we see Jesus say in John 12:48:

He that rejecteth me, and receiveth not my words, hath one that judgeth him: the word that I have spoken, the same shall judge him in the last day.

Notice in Revelations Jesus said "I will come" and when He does He expects His church to be ready, without spot or wrinkle, basically saying He wants them to fully be in love with Him.

The same God that was praising them and protecting them is the same one who said He would come and destroy them for sin.

Here's another example!

Revelations 2:18-26:

And unto the angel of the church in Thyatira write; These things saith the Son of God, who hath his eyes like unto a flame of fire, and his feet are like fine brass; I know thy works, and charity, and service, and faith, and thy patience, and thy works; and the last to be more than the first. Notwithstanding I have a few things against thee, because thou sufferest that woman Jezebel, which calleth herself a prophetess, to teach and to seduce my servants to commit fornication, and to eat things sacrificed unto idols. And I gave her space to repent of her fornication; and she repented not. Behold, I will cast her into a bed, and them that commit adultery with her into great tribulation, except they repent of their deeds. And I will kill her children with death; and all the churches shall know that I am he which searcheth the reins and hearts: and I will give unto every one of you according to your works. But unto you I say, and unto the rest in Thyatira, as many as have not this doctrine, and which have not known the depths of Satan, as they speak; I will put upon you none other burden. But that which ye have already hold fast till I come. And he that overcometh, and keepeth my works unto the end, to him will I give power over the nations.

Lets take a look at what happened here:

- He liked their faith
- He saw their works
- He saw their patience

Problem:

- God saw their sin, and they WOULDN'T REPENT for their sin

- He warned that HE, being Jesus, would kill them and their children if they didn't repent for their sin!

NON-REPENTED SIN WILL KILL YOU! Therefore you must read His word to see what sin is, and then repent for it!

Let's take another look at an end time church. This time we will dissect what God says to the church of Sardis in Revelations 3:1-5:

And unto the angel of the church in Sardis write; These things saith he that hath the seven Spirits of God, and the seven stars; I know thy works, that thou hast a name that thou livest, and art dead. Be watchful, and strengthen the things which remain, that are ready to die: for I have not found thy works perfect before God. Remember therefore how thou hast received and heard, and hold fast, and repent. If therefore thou shalt not watch, I will come on thee as a thief, and thou shalt not know what hour I will come upon thee. Thou hast a few names even in Sardis which have not defiled their garments; and they shall walk with me in white: for they are worthy. He that overcometh, the same shall be clothed in white raiment; and I will not blot out his name out of the book of life, but I will confess his name before my Father, and before his angels.

Let's take a closer look at what Jesus said:

- I know thy works
- He hadn't found their works PERFECT
- God wants them to go BACK and REPENT
- If they didn't, HE WOULD BLOT THEIR NAME OUT OF THE BOOK OF LIFE

Wow, this information is invaluable! God, who said in Exodus, that He would blot names out for sin, STILL in revelations is blotting names out for sin. In EACH example, the flaws that each church had are found in the first five books of the bible! All of those things are words that God told man not to do! Jesus is urging us to repent, which is to turn from a life of evil, which is the life of not loving Him back! This is the complete opposite from the false doctrine I hear consistently that Jesus finished the work and there is no more work for us to do. "There is nothing we can do to get salvation, God finished it at the cross." This is damaging to the body as we clearly see, WHAT WE DO MATTERS. As a matter of fact I outlined each time that God refers to judging man by what we do and this theme occurs 18 times in the book of Revelations alone! Man I thank God for His word. There won't be any surprises for those that know it.

Each of the examples investigated, we find sin as the sole reason for the separation. Get this, sin separates man from God. Turning from sin, mends the relationship. Staying in, or not knowing what sin is, doesn't help. His people are destroyed for a lack of knowledge, they don't get a pass for it. Look at what Isaiah has to say concerning sin and separation:

Isaiah 59:1-2:

> Behold, the Lord's hand is not shortened, that it cannot save; neither his ear heavy, that it cannot hear: but your iniquities have separated between you and your God, and your sins have hid his face from you, that he will not hear.

Sin separated man from God then and it does now. Because this is so important, let's find out what sin actually is. 1 John 3:4 says:

Whoever commits sin also commits lawlessness, and sin is lawlessness. We've been taught that sin is missing the mark. It is missing the mark, but the mark isn't your conscious, it's the laws of God. We can tell from the above scriptures that those churches and church-goers didn't acknowledge the commandments of God. Let's all strive NOT to be like them.

Lets also look at what Paul says about the lawless mindset in Romans the 8:5-8 chapter:

> For those who live according to the flesh set their minds on the things of the flesh, but those *who live* according to the Spirit, the things of the Spirit. For to be carnally minded *is* death, but to be spiritually minded *is* life and peace. Because the carnal mind *is* enmity against God; for it is not subject to the law of

God, nor indeed can be. So then, those who are in the flesh cannot please God.

The same way my wife can't cheat on me and please me, is the same way we can't disregard His commandments, which show us how to please Him, then turn around and say we make God happy. I can't make my wife happy the way I want to and neither can we make God happy the way we want too. It must be according to His word. See, our wives have a mouth, and in most cases it's a loud one ☺. Therefore her mate will know everything she feels. God is the same, it's His love language, which is outlined in His Word. We must read it! You won't know what He requires if you don't. Many people think the spirit of God will stop someone from sin, or make them feel bad for sin and that is rarely the case in the bible. One of the jobs of the Holy Spirit is to convince the world that they need Christ. That's just the first step in joining His covenant. Now we must act upon our beliefs and knowing how to do so requires reading His word. If we don't understand sin, then how can we ever turn from it? When you repent, in the spirit realm, the blood of Christ covers your from your sin and the blood sets you free. Therefore knowing what sin is should be a primary focus in the Christian church.

What if your pastor taught a message that God doesn't want you to wear make up, go to the movies and to never drink a sip of alcohol. The choir was rocking, the pastor was moving, and from your virgin eyes, it looked as if the Spirit of God was in the room. So you go to the altar and except Jesus as your Lord and Savior. You really didn't drink too much alcohol, had a wine for dinner or a martini when you went out with your girls. You didn't understand the no make up thing, but you did it, and you never went to the movies again. You started to become very involved in that church and you eventually became the prophet of that church. You worked a great job, which led you to start your own business, which took off and made so much money that you bought the church a new building. And to top all of that off, your mom was sick with cancer and you healed her in front of the whole congregation.

Then one day you died and woke up to see the face of Jesus. It's the white throne judgment aka judgment day and Jesus says "Hi." and you respond with a wave. He says according to Revelations that He will judge you according to your works, and starts to ask you about them. He says, "I see you prophesied, healed the sick, and built a church, but did you keep my words?" You say with a smile on your face, "Yes. I didn't go to the movies, didn't wear make up and stopped drinking. I went to church every Sunday, loved my neighbor as myself and loved you with all my heart, mind and soul." Then Christ responds, "Those were not my words. I told you in my Word to keep my commandments! Did you put other gods in my face, such as Ashoreth and Eostre, god's of Babylon? Did you keep idols around your home? Did you take my name and turn it into nothingness, did you keep my Sabbath day holy, did you..." and suddenly you stop Him and say, "What are you talking about, my pastor never preached this, I turned from my life of sin, I loved you!" And Christ responds, "You never knew what sin was. I loved you, but you never loved me back. Depart from me you worker of sin!" You stop Him and say, "WAIT, WHAT ABOUT THE BLOOD?" Jesus responds: "My blood was shed to cleanse man from repented sin. You never repented for your sins because you never knew what sin was to me, therefore, I never knew you." You yell back, "Well I knew YOU!" and then 1st John 2:4 scrolls in front of you; "And hereby we do know that we know him, if we keep his commandments."

As scary as this scenario may sound, this scenario is found all throughout the bible. Paul says in Romans 8:38-39:

For I am persuaded, that neither death, nor life, nor angels, nor principalities, nor powers, nor things present, nor things to come, Nor height, nor depth, nor any other creature, shall be able to separate us from the love of God, which is in Christ Jesus our Lord.

If we read this whole chapter we see that nothing will separate those that walk in the Spirit of God, with a law-keeping mindset. Take time and read it. For sinners it's a different story. Many times we hang our hat on God's love without understanding that a lack of loving God or not understanding God's love language, will separate us from Him. Because of unexplained scriptures like these, people feel like they know God and simply don't. Have you ever wondered how you can be sure that you are in Christ? The answer is found in 1ˢᵗ John 2:4-5:

> He that saith, I know him, and keepeth not his commandments,
> is a liar, and the truth is not in him. But whoso keepeth his
> word, in him verily is the love of God perfected: hereby <u>know
> we</u> that we are in him."

This is incredible information, rooted in wisdom and under-standing. John, the disciple whom Jesus loved, said obedience to His Word is how our love for God can be made perfect. John says, that this is our measuring stick, our checking point if you will. Then, above that, he says that if we think we know Him and don't keep His command-ments, we've lied, not only to others, but to ourselves.

Do you keep God's commandments?

I didn't before, but now I do. I've allowed myself to become an empty cup for the Lord and simply allowed Him and Him alone to fill it up with His words. I tell everyone to start off with the 10 command-ments and start to read His word, He'll propel you from there. There are other laws that God will judge us for, but the 10 commandments are a great start. Paul displayed the same mindset when He said in Romans 7:10-12:

> And the commandment, which was ordained to life, I found to
> be unto death. For sin, taking occasion by the commandment,
> deceived me, and by it slew me. Wherefore the law is holy, and

the commandment holy, and just, and good.

Paul said that the commandments of God slew him. Now Paul was most certainly alive when he wrote this, however, once Paul got the Word, his old life of sin died. Therefore Paul encourages us to die daily, become a living sacrifice, and to be a new creature in Christ Jesus. Allow His word to shape and govern your every move; this is the essence of being kingdom minded. Paul also says that this lifestyle leads to being a child of God in Romans 8:13-15:

For if ye live after the flesh, ye shall die: but if ye through the Spirit do mortify the deeds of the body, ye shall live. For as many as are led by the Spirit of God, they are the sons of God.

The word "Spirit" has many definitions, but we see Christ tells us in John 6:63 that His words are Spirit and are life. We also know that one of the jobs of the Holy Spirit is to bring His words to our remembrance and for this to be effective, we must know His word in order to remember it. Therefore Paul is telling us to live by Gods Words and not our flesh so that we may live. For if we are led by His word, then we are His children. Then if we are His children, THEN we are His joint-heirs, but it all starts with loving Him!

While upon this earth we are called to be ambassadors for Christ according to 2nd Corinthians 5:20. An Ambassador is one who has shifted their authority and their way of thinking over to the authority, feelings, and thoughts of their governing body. Our King is Jesus and this bible is our book of rules and opportunities. If we love Him, we are His children, if we don't He still shows us love, but its only a matter of time before total separation occurs, unless you turn from a life of sin. If you've read the whole bible you'll realize that most of it is about people who loved a life of sin more than a life with Him. Then our gracious God decides to take on the form of man and shed His blood to save the entire world. Then we realize that He's prepared a kingdom that will last forever, designed to hold those, that throughout all odds, endured to the end and chose to love Him back. In Revelations 22, the last chapter in the bible, Jesus says in verses 12-14:

"And, behold, I come quickly; and my reward is with me, to give every man according as his work shall be. I am Alpha and Omega, the beginning and the end, the first and the last. Blessed are they that do his commandments, that they may have right to the tree of life, and may enter in through the gates into the city. For without are dogs, and sorcerers, and whoremongers, and murderers, and idolaters, and whosoever loveth and maketh a lie."

Who's in?

The people who have faith in Him and kept His commandments.

Who's not?

People who broke the commandments of God and never repented for them.

(For understanding of how scriptures like "For Christ is the end of the law" fit into to loving God, please read the chapter Understanding Grace)

I use to always pray this prayer:

"God forgive me for the sins that I don't know about, and help me be obedient to the ones that I do."

I know many of you pray that as well. I pray to God that He answers them. However, His word is plain:

"My people are destroyed from a lack of knowledge." – Hosea 4:6

Right after that, in the same verse God says, "thou hast forgotten the law of thy God!" That means the His people, His church has forgotten what He requires, therefore they were living in non-repented sin, which means they weren't loving God back.

Let me show you the words of Jesus through David as He describes Himself in Proverbs 8:17,19-36:

I love them that love me; and those that seek me early shall find me. My fruit is better than gold, yea, than fine gold; and my revenue than choice silver. I lead in the way of righteousness, in the midst of the paths of judgment: That I may cause those that love me to inherit substance; and I will fill their treasures. The Lord possessed me in the beginning of his way, before his works of old. I was set up from everlasting, from the beginning, or ever the earth was. When there were no depths, I was brought forth; when there were no fountains abounding with water. Before the mountains were settled, before the hills was I brought forth: While as yet he had not made the earth, nor the fields, nor the highest part of the dust of the world. When he prepared the heavens, I was there: when he set a compass upon the face of the depth: When he established the clouds above: when he strengthened the fountains of the deep: When he gave to the sea his decree, that the waters should not pass his commandment: when he appointed the foundations of the earth: Then I was by him, as one brought up with him: and I was daily his delight, rejoicing always before him; Rejoicing in the habitable part of his earth; and my delights were with the sons of men. Now therefore hearken unto me, O ye children: for blessed are they that keep my ways. Hear instruction, and be wise, and refuse it not. Blessed is the man that heareth me, watching daily at my gates, waiting at the posts of my doors. For whoso findeth me findeth life, and shall obtain favour of the Lord. But he that sinneth against me wrongeth his own soul: all they that hate me love death.

This passage has summed up everything that we've learned.

- That Jesus was in the beginning
- That He is the one who dealt with man
- That He and His instructions are the way of Life
- That He loves those that love Him back!

Of course God loves the world, but there comes a time, as we've seen, that when we don't love Him back, He will destroy! His love remains with those that love Him back. Remember what He said in the flesh, in John 14:21:

He that hath my commandments, and keepeth them, he it is that loveth me: and he that loveth me shall be loved of my Father, and I will love him, and will manifest myself to him.

Follow the progression:

1. Keep His commandments
2. Those that love Him, keep His commandments
3. If you keep Jesus' commandments, the Father will love you
4. Jesus will love those that keep His commandments
5. If you do this, you will see God

No wonder why God said Wisdom was better than silver and gold. Wisdom will save your souls! I'm writing to you so you no longer have to pray a prayer that we can only hope works, or think your in a position that you're not in yet. Unlike much of our history, The Word of God is available now more than ever. Therefore we can study to show ourselves approved now more than ever. The problem lies in the doctrine of today. Is the bible really applicable? Is there even a law to follow? What about being gay and is the Sabbath still on the table? Can I eat anything I desire and is it ok with God? The truth is, we don't even question these things, because everyone thinks they love God and they already think they keep Jesus' commandments. Satan has done a mighty work amongst the leadership in Christianity, a mighty one! But fear not, His word is still here. You still have the opportunity to read His word and turn your life around. Check out what God says in Ezekiel 18:21-22:

> But if the wicked will turn from all his sins that he hath committed, and keep all my statutes, and do that which is lawful and right, he shall surely live, he shall not die. All his transgressions that he hath committed, they shall not be mentioned unto him.

That's right, the wicked has a chance. If you're wicked today, don't worry, everyone except Jesus was, you too have a chance to turn and live. That's what the blood is for. Now go and sin no more.

(Want to know how John 3:16 fits into this equation? Read the chapter, John 3:16 revealed)

Here are a few scriptures to help you along the way:

John 14:24 - He that loveth me not keepeth not my sayings: and the word which ye hear is not mine, but the Father's which sent me.

Matthew 5:48 - Be ye therefore perfect, even as your Father which is in heaven is perfect.

1 John 5:3 - For this is the love of God, that we keep his command-ments: and his commandments are not grievous.

Matthew 4:4 - Man shall not live by bread alone, but by every word that proceeds from the mouth of God

Mark 8:37-38 - What shall a man give in exchange for his soul? Whosoever therefore shall be ashamed of me and of my words in this adulterous and sinful generation; of him also shall the Son of man be ashamed, when he cometh in the glory of his Father with the holy angels.

Matthew 16:24-25- If any man will come after me, let him deny him-self, and take up his cross, and follow me. For whosoever will save his life shall lose it: and whosoever will lose his life for my sake shall find it.

1 John 3:7- Dear children, do not let anyone lead you astray. The one who does what is right is righteous, just as he is righteous.

James 4:7 - Submit yourselves therefore to God.

John 15:10-11 - If ye keep my commandments, ye shall abide in my love; even as I have kept my Father's commandments, and abide in his love. These things have I spoken unto you, that my joy might remain in you, and that your joy might be full.

Revelation 14:12 - Here is the patience of the saints: here are they that keep the commandments of God, and the faith of Jesus.

Revelation 12:17 - And the dragon was wroth with the woman, and went to make war with the remnant of her seed, which keep the commandments of God, and have the testimony of Jesus Christ.

James 2:17 - Even so faith, if it hath not works, is dead, being alone.

Side Note:

{Many say that works were for the Jews and not for Christ-like people living today. To briefly address this, I'd like to speak from the mind of God, which spoke through Isaiah in the 56th chapter. There, God lets us know that there is no division in the midst of His people. There isn't one law for the Jew and another one for the Gentile. When God allows the Gentiles and other nations into His "House of Prayer for All People", they ALL must do what pleases Him and that is to keep His commandments. This "House of Prayer for All People" Isaiah speaks of, didn't start until Jesus had already risen, some scholars say up to thirty years after the resurrection of Christ, starting with Cornelius in the book of Acts. This is the "New Testament" concept! Don't believe it, read revelations! We will be judged on the commandments of God. Peter, Paul, John and James as well as all of his disciples and followers had their hearts set on loving God back and so should we.}

See you in the next chapter...

Understanding Grace

*T*he GRACE of God! Wow, just thinking about it gives me the chills. 'THE ACT OF GRACE' is one of the top three, if not the top act recorded in the bible, but how many of us actually understand it?

Grace is two-fold; several times you'll read, "Grace be unto you" or "My grace is sufficient" which is saying nothing more than, God's favor or His kindness be unto you or God's favor is sufficient. Then we see the "GRACE OF GOD", that directly deals with God showing His favor and kindness towards man, by allowing Jesus to not only come to this dark world, but to shed His blood for the eradication of sins.

God's grace has always existed upon this world and still exists unto this day. However, there is a difference between being gracious towards somebody and the 'Act of Grace,' which is a one-time occurrence that will never be duplicated! There are many relevant questions that surround 'The Act' of Grace and we'll deal with those today:

- What is Grace
- Does Grace erase my need for works

- Was Grace only for the church
- What does God expect now that His 'Act' of Grace is finished

Let's investigate!

1 peter 1:10:

Of which salvation the prophets have enquired and searched diligently, who prophesied of the grace that should come unto you.

Various people in the Old Testament, like Noah, found the grace of God, however 'The Act' of Grace was something everyone looked forward to. From Adam, to Moses, to Job, to David, to the twelve sons of Israel, to Isaiah and Jeremiah, they all hoped that this 'Act' of Grace would come and give them the chance at eternal life in which they all strived for. Paul says in Ephesians 2:4-5:

But God, who is rich in mercy, for his great love wherewith he loved us, even when we were dead in sins, hath quickened us together with Christ, (by grace ye are saved;)

Notice a few key points here:

1. God loved us. This is the same love spoke of by Jesus in John 3:16; For God so loved the world, that He sent His son.
2. The reason God sent His son is because of the second point Paul makes, "We were dead in sins"

Paul and the rest of the bible let us know that "The wages of sin is death"! Your wages are what you earn. You go to work and your wages are the number you see on your paychecks. Well get this, the payment for sin is eternal damnation! It was the payment for David, for Moses, for Jacob, for Adam, for Eve, for Ruth, for Sampson, for Noah, for Isaiah and everyone else in this world. Why? Because everyone had sinned and even though some were washed in the blood of animals, Hebrews 10:4 tells us that the blood of animals CAN NOT take away sin. Therefore, the world was in a pickle!

BUT, GOD!

Romans 3:23-25:

> For all have sinned, and come short of the glory of God; being justified freely by his grace through the redemption *(ransom payment)* that is in Christ Jesus: Whom God hath set forth to be a propitiation *(calming)* through faith in his blood, to declare his righteousness for the remission *(pardon)* of sins that are past, through the forbearance *(patience)* of God.
>
> *(my words are in parentheses)*

Let's recap:

1. All have sinned, meaning everyone had a debt called death!
2. That debt has been paid by Jesus!

Yahshua's, being Jesus', blood has the ability to pardon sins. That's why Jesus says during 'The Last Supper'; "This is my blood, which is shed for the remission of sins." This is the good news! This is reason to shout! We don't have to die! But now that His blood is shed, grace has been established, what does that mean for us? How can we take hold to the not dying part?

A few things have to be considered:

1. Who did Jesus die for?

Hebrews 2:9 - But we see Jesus, who was made a little lower than the angels for the suffering of death, crowned with glory and honour; that he by the grace of God should taste death for every man.

Romans 5:15, Hebrews 2:8-10, Hebrews 5:19-21 tells us that Jesus died for every man. That means everyone that existed and everyone that is to exist. However, does this mean no one will die the eternal death of the lake of fire? And to be even plainer, does this mean everyone will make it into the kingdom of heaven? Let's investigate!

Revelations 20:12-15:

And I saw the dead, small and great, stand before God; and the books were opened: and another book was opened, which is the book of life: and the dead were judged out of those things which were written in the books, according to their works. And the sea gave up the dead which were in it; and death and hell delivered up the dead which were in them: and they were judged every man according to their works. And death and hell were cast into the lake of fire. This is the second death. And whosoever was not found written in the book of life was cast into the lake of fire.

Let's analyze! We see that God will judge people for their works, which provokes names to be blotted out of the book of life. We've learned in the *How to Love God* chapter that names get blotted out for sin. Therefore, the sinful workings of man gets their names blotted out!

Now this is very important; what have we learned so far?

1. The Act of Grace was Jesus Christ coming and dying for our sins!
2. He died for the whole world to get salvation!
3. Everyone doesn't get in!

Let's analyze some scriptures concerning Grace, and maybe it can shed some light on what we've learned.

Ephesians 1:7 - In whom we have redemption through his blood, the forgiveness of sins, according to the riches of his grace.

Colossians 1:14 - In whom we have redemption (recovery) through his blood, even the forgiveness of sins.

Romans 5:9 - Much more then, being now justified by his blood, we shall be saved from wrath through him.

Here's what we've gathered:
- God's grace is most certainly plentiful!
- It has the ability to redeem everyone!
- Its saves us from the lake of fire we just read about!
- It allows forgiveness for sin!

So, if I put two and two together, we would equate that people who didn't get into the kingdom of God, hadn't been forgiven for their sins. There are only three logical reasons I could think of for someone not to have their sins forgiven:
1) They didn't believe in this God and they just didn't care
2) They didn't know what sin was
3) They thought Grace replaced the need to live contrary to sin

Titus 2:11-12 says:

For the grace of God that bringeth salvation hath appeared to all men, Teaching us that, denying ungodliness and worldly lusts, we should live soberly, righteously, and godly, in this present world.

So Grace that leads to eternal life for all men doesn't deny the need of obedience towards God, rather it should teach us to be more obedient towards God! Why have we heard something different? Why have we heard that Grace cancels the need of works, and specifically, the works of the law- IT'S BECAUSE GRACE HAS! The question is, WHICH LAW HAS GRACE REPLACED?

Ephesians 2:8-10 sets the stage for our investigation:

> For by grace are ye saved through faith; and that not of your-selves: it is the gift of God: Not of works, lest any man should boast. For we are his workmanship, created in Christ Jesus unto good works, which God hath before ordained that we should walk in them.

Two things we see:

1) Man had nothing to do with Grace, which is Jesus' coming, dying and resurrecting
2) Man's individual nor collective works had anything to do with this GIFT given by God. God made sure of that, so that no man could boast about bringing Eternal Life back into the picture for all man. Only God and God alone is responsible
3) There's some good works and there's some works less desired

The other day I fell off my bike (I know right) and my cousin just had a baby so I decided to finish riding and headed to the hospital.

Because of my minor bruises, I went to talk to the nurse. I ran into a young lady who was reading 1st John. I said hello and then pointed to 1John 2:3-4 which reads:

And hereby we do know that we know him, if we keep his commandments. He that saith, I know him, and keepeth not his commandments, is a liar, and the truth is not in him. But whoso keepeth his word, in him verily is the love of God perfected: hereby know we that we are in him.

Immediately she closed her book and said, "No, I'm saved by grace, not the works of the law. No man is perfect, all is under sin, we're all sinners, God knows our heart and we'll all end up in heaven." I told her that every man has sinned, however Christ, Paul, James and John were adamant about us leaving a life of sin for a life of holiness. I showed her Matthew 5 where Christ says cut off your hand and pluck your eye out if it causes you to sin. I showed her in Matthew 5 that Christ said become perfect and in Revelations 3 that Christ was threating to send His church to the lake of fire because they weren't, unless they repent. I attempted to show her another place and she stopped me and said, "You don't get it do you? I'm saved by Grace!" I nodded my head and politely left out. It was then that I realized that most the Christian church reads over half their bible with little to no understanding of which Works God deems good and which Works God deems bad. The confusion stems from a heralded church figure named John Nelson Darby. Darby came up with the theory of dispensationalism and said that we as a church are under the dispensation of Grace; which is true. But then Darby proceeded to say, "We should abandon self-efforts to fulfill the law as a means to salvation!" Once Darby's theory was established in the 1800's, one hundred and twelve bible schools opened their doors and for the first time in history, the majority of the Christian church was taught that due to GRACE, they were released from the works of law of God. Again, this is true, but which works from what law are we released from?

The New Testament uses a general term "Law", however, in many cases it's referring to different laws found in the Old Testament. Each LAW, which there are several, hold commandments, statutes and decrees. For example, just say there are traffic laws. Under the traffic law you may have a commandment; don't run a red light. The decree may be; you would be fined if you run a red light. The statute may be; you can't run any stop signs, and or any signs or police or authority that prompts you to stop. Therefore we see the law holds things under it. Now, just as Traffic Laws aren't our only Law in the Law of the Land, the bible has several laws as well. If you don't know what the writer knew, which is the Old Testament, you would be extremely lost and read over half of your New Testament as well, with no understanding. But don't worry, we'll investigate!

The New Testament speaks on mainly, two different Laws, The Royal Law *(10 commandments and things that hang off of it)* and The Sacrificial Law *(law of animal sacrifice and the things that hang off of it)*. Each law has works under it. One set of works the New Testament abhors, the other set of works it praises. Let me show you several examples of this.

(The word WORKS is ergon in the Greek language. Sometimes transla- tors use ergon as deeds, doing well, or labor as well as works; we'll iden- tify when need be.)

Abhorred Works

- Galatians 2:21 - I do not frustrate the grace of God: for if righ- teousness come by the law, then Christ is dead in vain.

The Grace of God is worthless to the individual who continues to practice to works of the law Paul is speaking about, which we'll learn shortly.

- Titus 3:4-5- But after that the kindness and love of God our Saviour toward man appeared <u>not by works of righteousness</u> which we have done, but according to his mercy he saved us, by the washing of regeneration, and renewing of the Holy Ghost.

Jesus came, not by the works of man, but according to Mercy and His coming saved mankind. That's really all this passage is saying however many have been quoted in saying works have nothing to do with salvation.

- Romans 3:20- Therefore by the deeds of the law there shall no flesh be justified in his sight:

In God's sight, works WILL NOT make anyone just, meaning righteous.

- Galatians 2:16-Knowing that a man is not justified by the works of the law, but by the faith of Jesus Christ, even we have believed in Jesus Christ, that we might be justified by the faith of Christ, and not by the works of the law: for by the works of the law shall no flesh be justified.

Man IS NOT just in the sight of God by their works, but by faith.

- Romans 4:4-5- Now to him that worketh is the reward not reckoned of grace, but of debt. But to him that worketh not, but believeth on him that justifieth the ungodly, his faith is counted for righteousness.

By works, you're still under debt, your ransom is paid only through grace. Therefore if you don't do works and walk in faith, you are counted as righteous!

- Galatians 3:3,10 - Are ye so foolish? having begun in the Spirit, are ye now made perfect by the flesh? For as many as are of the works of the law are under the curse!

Those who work God's law are under a curse and are foolish.

- Romans 4:6 - Even as David also describeth the blessedness of the man, unto whom God imputeth righteousness without works.

David described a time that we would be just without doing the works of the law of God.

- Romans 11:6 - And if by grace, then is it no more of works: otherwise grace is no more grace. But if it be of works, then it is no more grace: otherwise work is no more work.

Because of Grace, there is not a need to do works!

These scriptures above are CLEAR! People who are trying to advance by the works of God's law are fools, cursed, and could never be made just or righteous. Now pay attention to *Works* being described in the complete opposite light!

Encouraged Works

- Titus 1:16 - They profess that they know God; but in works they deny him, being abominable, and disobedient, and unto every good work reprobate.

People will claim they know Christ, however their lifestyle will have lawless works. One that does the direct opposite of what God commanded us to do.

- Romans 2:13 - For not the hearers of the law are just before God, but the doers of the law shall be justified.

By obeying the law of God you are justified or righteous.

- 1 Corinthians 3:14 - If any man's work abide which he hath built thereupon, he shall receive a reward.

If you continue in good works, you will receive a reward.

- 2 Corinthians 9:8 - And God is able to make all grace abound toward you; that ye, always having all sufficiency in all things, may abound to every good work

Because Jesus came and died for us, we should desire to follow everything that He commanded.

- Galatians 5 - Now the works of the flesh are manifest, which are these; Adultery, fornication, uncleanness, wrath hatred lasciviousness, Idolatry, witchcraft, variance, emulations, seditions, heresies, Envyings, murders, drunkenness, revellings, and such like: of the which I tell you before, as I have also told you in time past, that they which do such things shall not inherit the kingdom of God.

Don't live according to the desire of your flesh, rather work the commandments of God. If you don't, you will not enter into His kingdom.

- Philippians 2:12 - Wherefore, my beloved, as ye have always obeyed, not as in my presence only, but now much more in my absence, work out your own salvation with fear and trembling.

Continue to work towards salvation, and do it with the fear of the Lord!

- Colossians 1:10 - That ye might walk worthy of the Lord unto all pleasing, being fruitful in every good work, and increasing in the knowledge of God;

Gaining knowledge, doing good works is pleasing unto God; therefore walk in this!

- Revelation 2:5 - Remember therefore from whence thou art fallen, and repent, and do the first works; or else I will come unto thee quickly, and will remove thy candlestick out of his place, except thou repent.

Do the first works commanded or else I will throw you into utter darkness. Therefore, please repent, which is turning back to obeying God.

- Revelation 2:23 - And I will kill her children with death; and all the churches shall know that I am he which searcheth the reins and hearts: and I will give unto every one of you according to your works.

God knows your heart, <u>but</u> He will judge you according to your actions, which is a bi-product of what your heart is really saying.

- Revelation 2:26 - And he that overcometh, and keepeth my works unto the end, to him will I give power over the nations:

For those that continue in my commandments, I will make Him reign with me during the thousand-year millennium period.

- Revelation 3:2 - Be watchful, and strengthen the things which remain, that are ready to die: for I have not found thy works perfect before God.

Jesus is asking them to get stronger, He's on His way and He's looking for a people without spot nor wrinkle.

- Revelation 20:13 - And the sea gave up the dead which were in it; and death and hell delivered up the dead which were in them: and they were judged every man according to their works.

Everyone will get judged according to what they do.

- Revelation 21:27 - And there shall in no wise enter into it any thing that defileth, neither whatsoever worketh abomination, or maketh a lie: but they which are written in the Lamb's book of life.

Nobody who breaks the commandments will enter into the kingdom of heaven.

- Jude 1:15 - To execute judgment upon all, and to convince all that are ungodly among them of all their ungodly deeds (works) which they have ungodly committed, and of all their hard speeches which ungodly sinners have spoken against him.

In the end, Christ will tell all ungodly people about their ungodly acts of lawlessness as well as dispel all ungodly doctrine.

- Revelations 2:22 - Behold, I will cast her into a bed, and them that commit adultery with her into great tribulation, except they repent of their deeds (works).

Repent for your sinful works or else God will punish you.

- Romans 2:5-7 - But after thy hardness and impenitent heart treasurest up unto thyself wrath against the day of wrath and revelation of the righteous judgment of God; Who will render to every man according to his deeds: To them who by patient continuance in well doing (works) seek for glory and honour and immortality, eternal life:

Seek everlasting life; therefore, keep doing good works, because God will judge you accordingly.

- James 2:14, 17 - What doth it profit, my brethren, though a man say he hath faith, and have not works? can faith save him? Even so faith, if it hath not works, is dead, being alone.

Faith in Jesus will not save you, you must accompany it with commandment keeping works.

- James 2:18 - Yea, a man may say, Thou hast faith, and I have works: shew me thy faith without thy works, and I will shew thee my faith by my works.

Your faith is determined by what type of works you're doing.

- James 2:24 - Ye see then how that by works a man is justified, and not by faith only.

By works man is justified, or made righteous!

- Matthew 7:21 - Not every one that saith unto me, Lord, Lord, shall enter into the kingdom of heaven; but he that doeth the will of my Father which is in heaven.

Everyone who calls upon the name of Jesus won't get into heaven. Only those that call upon Him and obey His will, which are His commandments, will enter in.

- 2 Thessalonians 2:17 - Comfort your hearts, and stablish you in every good word and work.

Establish yourself in speaking good words and walking in good works.

Now, we just read the 100% opposite scriptures on works, grace and faith. Here we see God wants us to repent for bad works and that good works lead to eternal life. A man is just or righteous by His works. Faith without these works are dead. Now is God crazy, The Word of God wrong, or do we simply need scriptural understanding? I'll choose door number three as well! (lol)

Works are an extension of a law. Works are the action of one following the commandments, decrees and statutes given to man by God. Therefore, each work is attached to a law. Lets quickly identify the different laws the New Testament harps on:

Hebrews 10:1-4:

> For the law having a shadow of good things to come, and not the very image of the things, can never with those sacrifices which they offered year by year continually make the comers thereunto perfect. For then would they not have ceased to be offered? because that the worshippers once purged should have had no more conscience of sins. But in those sacrifices there is a remembrance again made of sins every year. For it is not possible that the blood of bulls and of goats should take away sins.

Paul starts off, "FOR THE LAW", and then starts talking about sacrifices that had to be offered year-by-year, blood of bulls and goats etc. Which Law in the Old Testament, which Paul is drawing from, deals with sacrifices and animal blood? Which law was only a shadow or the schoolmaster of Christ's blood being shed, which was the good thing to come? The Sacrificial Law, aka The Law of Animal Sacrifice.

Let me give you some background on this Law:

- The Law of Animal Sacrifice was added because Israel wouldn't stop sinning.

Jeremiah 7:22-24:

> For I spake not unto your fathers, nor commanded them in the day that I brought them out of the land of Egypt, concerning burnt offerings or sacrifices: But this thing commanded I them, saying, Obey my voice, and I will be your God, and ye shall be my people: and walk ye in all the ways that I have commanded you, that it may be well unto you. But they hearkened not, nor inclined their ear, but walked in the counsels and in the imagination of their evil heart, and went backward, and not forward.

God said, He didn't tell them anything about a Sacrificial Law, I just told them to obey, but they didn't. And because God didn't want to destroy the world again, He implemented a system 430 years after the promise to Abraham, which starts to be explained in Exodus 28 and didn't come into fruition until Leviticus the 9ᵗʰ Chapter. On the contrary, the Royal Law, the 10 commandments decrees and statutes were orally spoken by God to Israel in Exodus the 20ᵗʰ chapter which was way before the institution of animal sacrifice found in Leviticus 9. With that understanding, lets establish which works are good vs. which works are no good by establishing which law is good vs. which one is no good.

Let's start in Galatians 3. Paul is scolding the Galatians, for what is perceived to be for keeping commandments such as the 10! Feel his words as we read them in Galatians 3:1-5:

O foolish Galatians, who hath bewitched you, that ye should not obey the truth, before whose eyes Jesus Christ hath been evidently set forth, crucified among you? This only would I learn of you, Received ye the Spirit by the works of the law, or by the hearing of faith? Are ye so foolish? having begun in the Spirit, are ye now made perfect by the flesh? Have ye suffered so many things in vain? if it be yet in vain. He therefore that ministereth to you the Spirit, and worketh miracles among you, doeth he it by the works of the law, or by the hearing of faith?

I mean Paul is laying them out! But why? What works are they keeping that would target a response such as this? The only way to correctly answer this is by correctly identifying the Law that Paul is referring to. Lets read verse 19:

Wherefore then serveth the law? <u>It was added</u> because of transgressions, till the seed should come to whom the promise was made.

Paul said why are you Galatians serving the law? The law that was added because of sin! Here's the million dollar question, which law was added because the people continued to sin? The LAW OF ANIMAL SACRIFICE!

Let's break this down even further. Paul tells us in Romans 5 that there is no sin when there is no law. Get this, Paul is saying in Galatians 3:19 that because ONE law was broken, ANOTHER law was added. The law that was added is the law Paul is scolding them for. Let's see his language towards this law in Galatians 3 so we can identify it in other scriptures:

- Its against faith – Galatians 3:2,5,12
- Its foolish to do - Galatians 3:1
- Those who do it are cursed – Galatians 3:10
- No man is justified by it – Galatians 3:11
- Christ has recovered, or redeemed us from this law – Galatians 3:13,19

Don't you just thank God for understanding? John Nelson Darby didn't understand and now has created a real mess in the Christian Church that God wants changed. With the understanding we just obtained we can read scriptures like these, with complete understanding:

Romans 10:4:

> For Christ is the end of the law for righteousness to every one
> that believeth.

Christ's death and resurrection is the end of The Law of Animal Sacrifice for everyone who believes that Christ came and shed His blood for His sins. Thinking that Christ is the end of every law would go directly against what Christ said from His very own mouth in Matthew 5:17-18:

> Think not that I am come to destroy the law, or the prophets: I
> am not come to destroy, but to fulfil. For verily I say unto you,
> Till heaven and earth pass, one jot or one tittle shall in no wise
> pass from the law, till all be fulfilled.

That word, fulfill, means to fill up like water being poured into an empty cup. Then Christ immediately starts filling up the Royal Law by saying; before I told you not to kill *(thou shalt not murder - 10 commandments)* now I'm telling you not to even be angry with your brother without cause! Before I told you not to commit adultery *(thou shalt not commit adultery - 10 commandments)* now I'm telling you whoever lusts after a woman as committed adultery in his heart and is guilty of it! This is adding to what was already there. Christ said, not one aspect of this law will be over until heaven and earth pass. Is heaven and earth still here? So then, Christ is not the end of every law is He? We learned in the previous *The Love Language of God* chapter that Loving God with all of our hearts and our neighbors as ourselves directly correlate to obeying the Royal Law. God wants us to keep His Royal Law and not to keep The Law of Animal Sacrifice.

Now lets look at another scripture found in Romans 3:20-21:

> Therefore by the deeds of the law there shall no flesh be justified in his sight: for by the law is the knowledge of sin. But now the righteousness of God without the law is manifested, being witnessed by the law and the prophets.

Paul is saying that killing animals for righteousness will no longer justify you in the sight of God, in past times it did. Sin separates man from God, however, the blood of animals would restore communication between God and man. We may not think so today, but back then, this was a tough sale for Paul. Paul was telling them that a system in which was kept for nearly 2000 years was over. A lamb was sacrificed daily and atonement for sins was kept annually in order for God to even deal with man. This was their comfort system, they knew nothing else! Now Faith was required. Now instead of physical blood, you had to believe the son of God, Jesus Christ's blood has eradicated your sin once repentance occurred. This was tough to stomach then, that's why Paul is so adamant in speech concerning it. Paul identifies which law he's referring to in verse 21. He says that righteousness outside of the law is here, being witnessed or wrote about by the prophets. Lets read one passage that backs up his statement:

Daniel the 9:26-27:

> And after threescore and two weeks shall Messiah *(Jesus)* be cut off, but not for himself: and the people of the prince that shall come shall destroy the city and the sanctuary; and the end thereof shall be with a flood, and unto the end of the war desolations are determined. And he shall confirm the covenant with many for one week: and in the midst of the week he shall cause the sacrifice and the oblation to CEASE, *(the law of animal sacrifice)* and for the overspreading of abominations he shall make it desolate.

(my words are in parentheses)

The sacrifice and oblation is referring to The Law of Animal Sacrifice. Daniel says it will be over by the cutting off or death of the Messiah, which is Jesus. Does the prophets say the Royal Law will be over? No! Nowhere in the first 39 books, nor the "lost books" even alludes to this. Remember what happened when Jesus died? Three of the four accounts tell us one major point that many simply have over looked. Let me show it to you:

Mark 15:37-38:

> And Jesus cried with a loud voice, and gave up the ghost. And the veil of the temple was rent in twain from the top to the bottom.

The moment Jesus died, the veil was tore in half! The veil is where they were instructed by God to put the blood of the animal in order for the High Priest to commune with God on behalf of himself and the people. God tore it as a sign that sacrificing is OVER as well as the priesthood that was added due to sin! Being obedient to the commandments of God is a quite different story. Look at what Paul has to say concerning it in Romans 6:1:

> What shall we say then? Shall we continue in sin, that grace may abound? God forbid. How shall we, that are dead to sin, live any longer therein?

Paul asks, should you live in sin or lawlessness simply because the 'Act' of Grace has occurred? His answer: GOD FORBID! He explains that we are to live dead or not according to sin aka the lust of our flesh. Look what else he says in verses 6-8 of the same chapter:

> Knowing this, that our old man is crucified with him, that the body of sin might be destroyed, that henceforth we should not serve sin. For he that is dead is freed from sin. Now if we be dead with Christ, we believe that we shall also live with him.

We are suppose to be dead from a life of sin which is defined in the bible in 1 John 3:4 as breaking Gods commandments. This, along with faith in Jesus, will usher us into eternal life, thus living with God forever and ever. This is why Paul makes this powerful statement in Romans 8:7-8:

The carnal mind is enmity against God: for it is not subject to the law of God, neither indeed can be. So then they that are in the flesh cannot please God.

Lawlessness can not, will not and won't ever be pleasing to God. Peter writes to us and tells us that Paul's writings are hard to understand and will lead those that are unlearned in the scriptures to eternal damnation in 2nd Peter 3:16. This book just helped you get the understanding that you've been praying for. Don't harden your heart, rather be thankful; God has answered you!

James 1:12-16:

Blessed is the man that endureth temptation: for when he is tried, he shall receive the crown of life, which the Lord hath promised to them that love him. Let no man say when he is tempted, I am tempted of God: for God cannot be tempted with evil, neither tempteth he any man: But every man is tempted, when he is drawn away of his own lust, and enticed. Then when lust hath conceived, it bringeth forth sin: and sin, when it is finished, bringeth forth death. Do not err, my beloved brethren.

Please do your part in spreading this word to the world.

See you in the next chapter...

The 4 Keys to Unlocking Love

*G*I Joe taught me one of the most important lessons that I've learned to date. He ended his program saying, "knowing is half the battle." Wow, how true is that! Knowing that we should love God and loving God are two completely separate entities. Knowing is only half the battle, the other half takes action. Many people get married without understanding that the wedding was only the beginning. That marriage must be built and so should your relationship with God. Christ says in Matthew 11:29, "Take my yoke upon you, and learn of me." A yoke isn't just hanging on the neck of an ox for decoration; the yoke was used when the ox was ready to work. Christ says take on my work, my job is light, and it's not burdensome or a waste of time.

Then Christ immediately says, "learn of me!" Every job you ever got should have given you an Operations Manual explaining tasks required of you. God's operation manual is His word. Just say, you go to work one day and you wear shorts. Nothings wrong with wearing shorts, right? Wrong! Your operation manual says if you wear shorts you will immediately be fired. Your excuse is, "I didn't know." Their response would be, "It's in the manual!" God's manual, which is the bible, is the foundation of your relationship towards Him. Therefore we must create our relationship by learning of Him and applying what we've learned.I use to say, "I know I don't keep the commandments, but I love Christ with my heart, so I'm sure I'll get in." That's nowhere in the bible. Nothing in the bible even alludes to this. Remember in the previous chapter, the people get separated by God for not learning of Him and/or learning of Him and not doing. God said through the mouth of James in the 4th chapter 8th verse "Draw nigh to God, and he will draw nigh to you." He's saying, move closer to me, and I will move closer to you. God wants to actually get closer to you. Think about that for a second. God, the creator of all heaven and earth, wants to be close with little old you. That within itself is amazing. But just like you, when you pursued your boyfriend or girlfriend, husband or wife, in order for the relationship to evolve, TIME had to be spent. You wanted to see them, to talk to them, hold them, to read their letters, texts or emails and for them to read yours, you wanted that person's time; and God is no different. <u>YOU NEED TIME WITH GOD and GOD NEEDS TIME WITH YOU</u> in order to make your relationship more effective. I suggest that you start off with 30 minutes a day with God. Take 15 minutes and read His word, then take the other 15 minutes and pray, praise, and meditate. Don't know what to pray for? Don't worry, you're not alone. Pray His will be done. Pray for your family. Have a conversation with God about what you're going through. Ask for instructions of wisdom; He will answer you. Take some time and meditate, seeing your end from the beginning. Then start calling things that are not as though they were. Start confessing you're in love with God daily. You might not be there yet, it's ok, you're working towards it and the more you work the hotter you'll become. In Matthew 7:7 Christ says:

Ask, and it shall be given you; seek, and ye shall find; knock, and it shall be opened unto you: For every one that ask receive; and he that seek find; and to him that knock it shall be opened.

You have to ask, you have to seek and you have to knock in order to obtain a real relationship with God. It's impossible to have one any other way.

During your prayer and reading time, four things must be developed and then exercised in your everyday life. Submission, Trust, Communication and Vision. These are the 4 keys that unlock love. There is no love without all of them combined in every real relationship that exists and it is no different with a relationship with God.

The first key that must be established in this formula is submission; which is also known as surrendering all, trading in your ways for His ways, your thoughts for His thoughts. Without submission none of the other keys will work and neither will your goal to become hot for the one that is hot for you.

Try to communicate with someone who doesn't submit. The conversation will go something like this:

God – Terry, turn those lights off.

Terry – I love you God. (no movement)

God – Terry, open that window.

Terry - I love you God. (no movement)

Terry is getting instruction from God and not moving an inch. He's sitting on his knees saying He loves God, but won't do what God asked Him. The mindset of submission must be established during communication with God or God's communication toward you will start to become null and void in your life.

Try trusting someone without submission. I like to use the 'fall back into my arms' method to validate this point. When someone asks you to fall back, you must mentally let go of your will and submit solely to what you hear. Without the mindset of submission one will never live by every word that proceeds out the mouth of God. You have to trust, and submission is the root of that.

What about vision? Let me show you an example of vision without submission.

God – Erik, teach the word.

Erik – God, I want to be the next Puffy.

God – Erik, teach the word.

Erik – God, I want to be the next Puff Daddy.

We're at a standstill and God can't move on my behalf. Look at Paul on the road to Damascus. He was on his way to do what he thought was the will of God. Yahshua showed up and Paul's plans did a complete 360 because he submitted to God's plan for his life instead of his own.

Submission is a mindset that The Word of God harps on. Commandments, laws, love the Lord, and love your neighbor mean the same thing, submit! Surrender all! Give yourself away! Another term that Paul uses is becoming "a living sacrifice!" Romans 12:1 says:

I beseech you therefore, brethren, by the mercies of God, that ye present your bodies a living sacrifice, holy, acceptable unto God, which is your reasonable service.

Becoming the living dead in order to have Christ alive in you, that's what Paul is talking about. Paul calls this our reasonable service. The lukewarm submits sometimes. God's way, then my way, God's way, then my way. That is the very thing Paul is urging us to get rid of. Christ came to destroy the works of the devil and the devil's job is to keep you away from the mindset of submission towards God.

Who's going to win?

Did you know that once you've said yes to Christ, you have agreed to die to your old ways and adopt the ways of Christ? That IS what being a Christian (Christ Like) or Israel (God's people) is all about.

Paul explains this process through the illustration of baptism in Romans 6:3-7 Paul says:

> Know ye not, that so many of us as were baptized into Jesus Christ were baptized into his death? Therefore we are buried with him by baptism into death: that like as Christ was raised up from the dead by the glory of the Father, even so we also should walk in newness of life.

A new life is supposed to begin in us. Didn't you hate your old one anyway? (lol) Well, the way to truly get a new one is to spiritually die the death from your old one. Paul says in 1ˢᵗ Corinthians 15:31 "I die daily!" When something is dead, there is no more struggle, there is no more thought, nor craving towards that past desire, It's DEAD! That's the attitude we must have if we plan to be alive in Christ. That's why 1 John 3:6 says:

> Whosoever abideth in him sinneth not.

Can you imagine living the rest of your life without sin? Walking according to every word that proceedeth out of the mouth of God, everyday? Knowing His commandments and actually living them? If you can, then also imagine this, living a life in which everything you touch prospers and all that is around you is blessed. When you pray, God responds! When you talk, mountains move. And even when trials come, you know they're from the hand of God to purge out the impurities in you that still may remain; so that too is ok. That is the life of the righteous. That's the life of the man or woman who has died daily!

The greatest act of love is DYING, so that another may LIVE! Many know that Jesus' death enabled us to live but do you also know that your death to sin enables others to live as well? Its true, Noah's death to sin saved his family. Paul's death to sin enabled 2/3rds of the New Testament to be written. When you die to the ways of this world, God will start to use you to save the rest of this world. Consider the life of the non-surrendered. Think about Saul's lack of submission when he kept the Amalekite King alive along with the choice stock in 1st Samuel 15. Saul had his chest stuck out and hands raised high as if he had done the will of God, but he hadn't. Saul said, "I have performed the commandment of the LORD!" with his mouth, but Saul's actions were completely opposite. God was angry with Saul and upset that he was the King of Israel, simply because Saul didn't like to submit. Yahweh removed His anointing and later replaced him with a young shepherd named David, simply due to a lack of submission. Proverbs 16:25 says:

There is a way that seemeth right unto a man, but the end thereof are the ways of death.

The only way that you know is when you decide to submit unto His word, finding the very will God has for your life.

Here are some scriptures to help you along the way.

Galatians 5:24 - And they that are Christ's have crucified the flesh with the affections and lusts.

Matthew 16:23-25 - "Then said Jesus unto his disciples, If any man will come after me, let him deny himself, and take up his cross, and follow me. For whosoever will save his life shall lose it: and whosoever will lose his life for my sake shall find it."

John 15:10 - If ye keep my commandments, ye shall abide in my love; even as I have kept my Father's commandments, and abide in his love.

John 15:12-15 - This is my commandment, That ye love one another, as I have loved you. Greater love hath no man than this, that a man lay down his life for his friends. Ye are my friends, if ye do whatsoever I command you. Henceforth I call you not servants; for the servant knoweth not what his lord doeth: but I have called you friends.

Matthew 16:24 - Then said Jesus unto his disciples, If any man will come after me, let him deny himself, and take up his cross, and follow me.

Psalm 18:44 - As soon as they hear of me, they shall obey me: the strangers shall submit themselves unto me.

James 4:7 - Submit yourselves therefore to God. Resist the devil, and he will flee from you.

John 10:17 - Therefore doth my Father love me, because I lay down my life, that I might take it again.

Now that you understand the importance of submission, we can talk about Trust, Communication, and Vision. The first of these last three we'll start off with Vision.

Habakkuk 2:2-4 says to write the vision down and to make it plain upon tables so he that reads it can run with it. In many marriages, people say vows. The vows that we speak are futuristic confessions that are planned to complete their vision of an everlasting marriage with their mate. You want your spouse to love you if you are sick, love you if you are broke, love you no matter the situation and nine times out of ten, your mate responds with the words "I Do". Well in this Christian life, our goal is to be "Christ Like". He lived full of provision. He was able to call things that were not as though they were. He walked in His calling, healing all those that were in need. He died, as we should, daily. He also ascended unto the throne, entering into the kingdom of Heaven, spending eternity with The Father. As a Christian we should aspire to do the same.

We've read in the previous chapter that God blots names out The Book of Life due to sin. Therefore, if the kingdom of heaven is your long-term goal, living dead to sin should be your short-term goal. Proverbs 29:18 says, "Where there is no vision, the people perish: but he that keepeth the law, happy is he." When you're dead to the world, the world no longer lives in you. God has it set up, where if we do it HIS way, all of our desires will be met. That's why Jesus preached The Kingdom of God. John preached The Kingdom of God. If you do what it takes to get into the kingdom of God, every blessing you'll ever need will come your way. We don't serve the god of money, we serve the God of provision! And when God is in the mix, provision is always met according to His will. Therefore, keep your vision on His kingdom and the vision you have for success will follow.

Many don't know this, but we serve an 'If and Then' God. If we do, His commandments, Then we'll reap the rewards. No blessing in the bible is outside of a commandment followed, not even one. For example, do you know how to become the head and not the tail? Do you know how the bible says to be blessed in the city and blessed in the field? Do you know how to delight thyself in the Lord so He can give you the desires of your heart? I'm sure you've heard these promises but have you heard that these promises are a direct result of keeping the 10 commandments, decrees and statutes that hang off of them? That's what the bible says. Keeping the commandments of God in Christ Jesus, equates to the eternal life that we all have a vision of. Our minds must be stuck on ETERNAL LIFE with the Lord. Set that as the light at the end of the tunnel, then you will start to see all the provisions of God along the way.

I often tell my friends that you must see yourself as a child of God before you can truly become a child of God. VISION! You must see yourself loving and giving to those that hate you, before you can actually live it. VISION! You must see yourself walking and talking by faith. VISION! VISION! VISION! That's why Joshua 1:8 says that if you meditate on the Word of God, see it back and forth in your mind, your way shall be prosperous and you will have good success. Vision is the key! Show me the man who doesn't envision his success and I'll show you a man who's headed for destruction. Without vision, Moses couldn't split the Red Sea. Without vision Paul would have given up or stuck with tent making. Without vision Yahshua wouldn't have said, "Not my will, but thy will!" Vision equals Freedom!

Mark 11:23 says:

> "For verily I say unto you, That whosoever shall say unto this mountain, Be thou removed, and be thou cast into the sea; and shall not doubt in his heart, but shall believe that those things which he saith shall come to pass; he shall have whatsoever he saith."

But how? How can we get the word so deep in our hearts that the realm of doubt can no longer touch it? How can we believe the things we actually say? How can we Let God Be True and every man a liar? With vision! Meditate on His word, His laws, His promises and His thoughts toward you, DAY AND NIGHT! When you do this, you create a mental vision in your head, backed by faith from the word of God, THEN your tongue will frame God's will around every aspect of your life. Then, nothing shall be impossible to you! Then, you can call things that are not as though they were and they shall be....only then! You have to envision the outcome when you have no income! You must see the mountain gone, while it's standing in your face! You must walk by Faith and not by sight! This is actually what God requires of you. Before you start running a race, start envisioning the finish line. A good runners mind is set on the finish line, nothing else. Not the person to the right or to the left, just the finish line. The marathon runner envisions the end before he takes his first step. The runner knows it's going to be a long, hard, challenging road, but they're ready, focusing on the finish! Consider the hurdler; He rarely notices the roadblocks ahead of him, he simply leaps over them. If you want to cross the finish line to God, keep your mind set on the vision of being next to God and that will keep you on the path that is narrow. Here are some scriptures to help you along the way.

Hebrews 12:1 - Wherefore seeing we also are compassed about with so great a cloud of witnesses, let us lay aside every weight, and the sin which doth so easily beset us, and let us run with patience the race that is set before us,

Matthew 10:22 - And ye shall be hated of all men for my name's sake: but he that endureth to the end shall be saved.

Psalm 37:23 - The steps of a good man are ordered by the LORD: and he delighteth in his way.

John 13:1 - Jesus knew that his hour was come that he should depart out of this world unto the Father, having loved his own which were in the world, he loved them unto the end.

John 10:17 - Therefore doth my Father love me, because I lay down my life, that I might take it again.

Luke 13:24 - Strive to enter in at the strait gate: for many, I say unto you, many will seek to enter in, and shall not be able.

Another key that we need in order to unlock love is TRUST. God gives us the order of things in Psalms 37:3 saying, "Trust in the LORD, and do good; so shalt thou dwell in the land, and verily thou shalt be fed." Trust is the first step in becoming good and being good is the step before inheriting the prosperity of God. If you want to win the battle in your mind, commit yourself to study, and trust in the Word of God. If you want to forgive, focus on trusting the one that is worthy of it. So many times we trust man, when we should wholly put our trust in the creator of man; God! When you are in a firm relationship and have allowed God to be your guide, you must know that He has your best interest at heart at all times. God does take us through storms and a good example of this is Job. But even in Job's state, he trusted that God was up to something. You may not figure it out at first, but if you trust in the Lord, you'll know that He has your overall best interest in mind.

A friend of mine was arrested and was sentenced to house arrest a few years ago. At first he was down, but after a while he started to trust that the Lord knew best. Now that he is off of house arrest, he'll be the first to tell you that being on house arrest was the best thing that could have ever happened to him. It enabled him to revitalize his relationship with his children, his business and most importantly, his God. We must maintain the mindset of trust even in our darkest hour. When you've properly submitted unto God, trusting Him becomes easier. When you've surrendered and have become clay, what can move you? We must learn to cultivate a mindset of trust towards the God we serve.

Consider Joseph, who went from being left for dead by his brothers, to being sold into slavery, to being falsely accused, to being imprisoned, to being forgotten, to being the lead official in a country called Egypt. MINDSET! Consider Abraham, when the Lord told him to sacrifice Isaac or when Jesus endured the cross. Or what about the Shunammite woman who refused to accept the death of her son because she deemed the God who promised her worthy! MINDSET! MINDSET! MINDSET! Every one of these children of God fixed their minds on trust and neither circumstance, nor situation could move it. Even when Job lost it all, because of his relationship with God, he trusted in Yahweh our Lord and God gave him a double portion of everything he lost. We must follow their example of TRUST if we want the same results that these people obtained. Here are a few scriptures to digest concerning trust in our Lord.

Proverbs 3:5 - Trust in the LORD with all thine heart; and lean not unto thine own understanding.

Isaiah 55:9 - For as the heavens are higher than the earth, so are my ways higher than your ways, and my thoughts than your thoughts.

Psalm 64:10 - The righteous shall be glad in the LORD, and shall trust in him

Proverbs 28:25 - He that is of a proud heart stirreth up strife: but he that putteth his trust in the LORD shall be made fat.

Last but certainly not least is communication. In 2005, lack of communication was the #1 reason for divorce in the United States of America! How can a relationship between you and God exist without true communication? It cannot! Some of you are exactly as I was: constantly scrambling for time to even speak with God; and when I finally did, I had no clue of what to say. Then others of you are like my close friend, who had no idea that God even wanted to communicate with him. Time in prayer and in His word is essential for a true relationship with God. What real relationship can survive off of an email once every blue moon, a random text once a month, or a two-hour visit once a week? For a distant friend, that's fine. Even with some close friends that's fine (lol). But what about your mate, your soul-mate? What about the one whom you love? Soon you'll realize that type of time is insufficient and that relationship will not last if something doesn't change and change fast. I was reading the book of Jasher the other day, about how much time Enoch spent with God. Even though Jasher isn't a part of the 66 books, it's quoted in Joshua and 2nd Samuel, so I read it and was fascinated by the type of committed time Enoch spent with God. Even when you look at Moses, 40 days after 40 days, Joshua not leaving the tent of meetings before he became the leader of Israel or Jesus and how he went away day in and day out talking to the Lord. Communication with God is essential if you plan on loving God. You will never be able to know someone you don't communicate with, it's impossible!

David says in Psalm 5:

> Give ear to my words, O LORD, consider my meditation. Hearken unto the voice of my cry, my King, and my God: for unto thee will I pray. My voice shalt thou hear in the morning, O LORD; in the morning will I direct my prayer unto thee.

We have to make time for God if we want God to make time for us. He can't be our spare tire; he needs to be our steering wheel. Fasting, praying, meditation and reading those "little sticky notes" called the books of the bible; this is how we communicate with our Lord. He also says in His word that He is the Shepherd and His sheep shall know His voice. I encourage you to find the voice of the Lord today by reading the words He left for you in His Holy Bible! One of the key jobs of the

Holy Spirit is to bring all things unto your remembrance, but if you don't know His word, what can the Set-Apart Spirit actually do for you? Nothing. Carve time out for the Lord and He will carve out a covering over you and your entire household. Here are some scriptures that will help you along the way.

Joshua 10:14 - And there was no day like that before it or after it, that the LORD hearkened unto the voice of a man: for the LORD fought for Israel.

John 10:27 - My sheep hear my voice, and I know them, and they follow me.

Jeremiah 25:36 - A voice of the cry of the shepherds, and an howling of the principal of the flock, shall be heard: for the LORD hath spoiled their pasture.

John 10:4-6 - And when he putteth forth his own sheep, he goeth before them, and the sheep follow him: for they know his voice. And a stranger will they not follow, but will flee from him: for they know not the voice of strangers.

Psalms 37:23 - The steps of a good man are ordered by the LORD: and he delighteth in his way.

See you in the next chapter...

John 3:16 Revealed

Matthew 7:13-14:

Enter ye in at the strait gate: for wide is the gate, and broad is the way, that leadeth to destruction, and many there be which go in thereat: Because strait is the gate, and narrow is the way, which leadeth unto life, and few there be that find it.

*S*alvation is available for everyone, but the bible is clear, only few will obtain it. This book I've written is simply a guide, giving you understanding, erasing non-biblical rhetoric from your minds, so that YOU can READ freely. One thing I learned early in my bible studying days is that the bible answers itself. Of course the WHY'S of the bible aren't always explained; rather they are there to let us into the mindset of God. Remember His ways and thoughts are higher than ours and it's ok to not understand them sometimes. However, when it comes to doctrine, ALL of the answers are there. Peter tells us in 2nd Peter 1:20 that there is no "private interpretation" of the scriptures. God's answers are His answers, period! The Greeks theologized everything and now you have several different doctrines that are extremely far from the doctrine of Jesus Christ. If you want to know the answer, GOD set it up where if you keep reading, you'll FIND it. Theology is based on, what WE THINK, our minds should be governed by what HE SAYS!

With that in mind I want to take a look at the most popular scripture known to mankind, John 3:16:

For God so Loved The World, that He gave His Only Begotten Son, that Whosoever Believeth in Him should Not Perish, but have Everlasting Life.

Of course this is true, but what is it really saying? Can anyone merely say, "I believe that Jesus is the Son of God" and have everlasting life?

In this chapter I want to show you that confessing with your mouth and believing in your heart is the first step to becoming a Christian. The next step is living it and that's what belief is all about. Romans 10:17 says, "Faith cometh by hearing and hearing the Word of God." but if you don't practice what you've heard/read, then your faith becomes dead. James describes it as a man who looks at himself in the mirror then walks away forgetting how he looked. We must look at His word and then *Live* His word. Not doing so is equivalent to me saying I'm in a Fraternity when I'm not. Why say I'm an Alpha if I've never learned the meaning behind being an Alpha? Never found out what being an Alpha requires? Never have denied my flesh and submitted to authority, but I walk around with Alpha gear on everyday and brand my body with the Alpha symbols? Now when a real Alpha man comes to me, I don't know the secret hand shake and nor can I truly answer any questions concerning what it takes to become an Alpha man, my true identity will be exposed and this is what Christ will do to many "Christians" on judgment day. He will say, "I heard you say you believe, but what did your life say?" "I know you claimed to be a part of my group but did you read, adhere to and minister my requirements to others." It means nothing to walk and talk Jesus everyday without knowing and doing what it requires to *Live* Jesus everyday.

Consider Judas, Jesus' boy, one of His twelve best friends. He walked with Jesus everyday. He talked about Jesus everyday. He healed people, he cast out demons, baptized, yet and still Judas betrayed Jesus. The scripture says that it is better for him to have never been born. Why? He talked Jesus, he hung with people who loved Jesus, but Judas didn't live Jesus. Consider Ananias and Sapphira. They heard about Jesus. They got excited and became part of the first church of Acts. They even sold their land with the intentions of giving a portion of their money to the movement. In our society they would be esteemed, but God killed them, simply for attempting to deceive the Spirit of God. They talked Jesus, but didn't live Jesus.

Acknowledging Jesus or having faith in Jesus is great. Through Him you can truly do all things. But faith without works is dead. Faith in Christ is like having a fancy remote control. It looks good, it's a great piece to show off in the home, but what good is the remote without the batteries. James says faith without works is dead. Your faith needs batteries. Remember what Jesus said in Matthew 7:21:

Not every one that saith unto me, Lord, Lord, shall enter into the kingdom of heaven; but he that <u>doeth the will of my Father</u> which is in heaven.

Again, faith without batteries is dead! Consider even the angels. Luke 4:33-34 says:

And in the synagogue there was a man, which had a spirit of

an unclean devil, and cried out with a loud voice, Saying, Let us

alone; what have we to do with thee, thou Jesus of Nazareth?

Art thou come to destroy us? I know thee who thou art; the

Holy One of God.

Two things in these scriptures stick out like a sore thumb.

1) The demon knew that one day it would perish

2) The demon knew that Jesus was the Son of God.

That fact that the demon knew who Jesus was didn't earn him a spot in the Kingdom of Heaven. Rather, his knowing without doing is what made that angel fall from an angel of light to a demon of darkness.

So what does BELIEF really mean?

Lets take a look at the Israelites in the wilderness. The New Testament says in Hebrews 3 that they didn't enter into the promise land because of UNBELIEF. Follow me on this...The Israelites SAW every miracle in Egypt. They SAW God pour manna down from heaven. They SAW the Red Sea split and personally walked on dry ground. They went to church once a week and MOSES was their pastor. The whole nation heard God speak audibly while they were at Mt. Sinai, 70 of the elders ate with Yahweh the Son Himself; they saw more of God than most of us ever will. According to American standards, THEY BELIEVED! So why were they considered non-believers? Joshua 5:6 says:

> For the children of Israel walked forty years in the wilderness, till all the people that were men of war, which came out of Egypt, were consumed, because they obeyed not the voice of the LORD.

They were considered non-believers because they didn't OBEY. Their feet didn't match what they'd heard. Their mind didn't submit to what they'd read. It was about God with their mouth but it was all about themselves with their actions.

Obedience = Belief

God doesn't consider anyone a believer who doesn't obey what he or she claims to believe. Remember how Matthew 7 describes a body of people who prophesied, who laid hands on the sick, and do many wonderful things in God. This doesn't sound like a people who didn't confess Christ and believe in Jesus according to our standards of belief. The next scripture says, "Depart from me, ye workers of Sin." Remember 1 John 3:4 "Sin is transgressing His laws." The Israelites broke them, the New Testament church broke them, and we see from the Book of Revelations that He warns His end time church to stop breaking them. Sin makes a person a non-believer in His eyes. Therefore when Jesus said, "Whosoever believeth in Him shall not perish." He meant the person whose belief – equaled - action. Christ is looking for the believer who would pick up his cross and *follow* Him, not just the man who said He believed, then lived in sin. With that understanding, let's delve into John 3:16:

For God so loved the world, that he gave his only begotten Son, that whosoever believeth in him should not perish, but have everlasting life.

Many stop here, but if we finish reading Jesus' thought we see that belief equaled obedience towards His commandments. John 3:18 says this:

He that believeth on him is not condemned *(guilty):* but he that believeth not is condemned already, because he hath not believed in the name of the only begotten Son of God.

The scripture first says if you believe you shall not perish. Then, it says if you believe you are not condemned. So if we can find WHO'S CONDEMNED then we can reverse it and further establish WHO BELIEVES! Lets journey to Romans 8:1:

There is therefore now no condemnation to them which are in Christ Jesus, who walk not after the flesh, but after the Spirit.

Paul uses the word "walk" which directly correlates to action. He says those, which are condemned, walk in the flesh and those that walk after the spirit or follow the instructions of God, are not guilty. Let's scroll down to verses 5-7:

"For they that are after the flesh do mind the things of the flesh; but they that are after the Spirit the things of the Spirit. For to be carnally minded is death; but to be spiritually minded is life and peace. Because the carnal mind is enmity (hostile) against God: for it is not subject to the law of God, neither indeed can be."

Meaning that the carnal, fleshly mind, has walked away from the laws or the commandments of God and does what IT sees fit and not what HE sees fit.

Let's continue to verse 8:

So then they that are in the flesh cannot please God.

So can the man that says "I believe" yet walks in the flesh please God? No! However, let us see if this adds up to the remainder of what Jesus said in John 3. Lets look at John 3:19:

"And this is the condemnation *(Here are they that are condemned)*, that light is come into the world, *(Jesus has come)* and men loved darkness rather than light, *(but man has loved satan's way more than Gods)* because their <u>deeds</u> were evil."
(my words are in parenthesis)

How does one show which side they're on? By the deeds they do. Is it by saying which side your on? According to Jesus, it's by living what side you're on. Let me show you another example of this in John the 8th chapter. Jesus says:

> 33They answered him, We be Abraham's seed, and were never in bondage to any man: how sayest thou, Ye shall be made free? 34Jesus answered them, Verily, verily, I say unto you, Whosoever committeth sin is the servant of sin. 39They answered and said unto him, Abraham is our father. Jesus saith unto them, If ye were Abraham's children, ye would do the works of Abraham. 41Ye do the deeds of your father. 44Ye are of your father the devil, and the lusts of your father ye will do. He was a murderer from the beginning, and abode not in the truth, because there is no truth in him. When he speaketh a lie, he speaketh of his own: for he is a liar, and the father of it.

Jesus alludes that obedience equals ownership. Who you obey is who owns you. God or satan, satan or God? It's a decision that must be made daily for the rest of our lives. Lets get back to John 3:20:

> For every one that doeth evil hateth the light, neither cometh to the light, lest his deeds should be reproved.

If doing evil is how you hate Jesus, then how do you love Him? Remember what the scripture referenced in the above chapter? "If you love ME, keep my commandments." - Jesus in John 14:15.

Jesus says out of His mouth, that if you love Me, want to live for me, want to spend eternal life with me, ACT!

Believing with your heart and confessing with your mouth is the first step, but that is just the beginning. Your deeds equal life and life equals belief and the deeds you must adhere to are the commandments of the Lord. This is why satan's agenda to the world was to have the people misunderstand John 3:16. Only if satan could get the people to live contrary to the commandments of God and never repent for it. Only if he could make them believe they were believers even if they lived a life contrary to His commandments. Only if he could take the ingredients for everlasting life out of the church. Only if he could have them say they love Jesus and know Jesus without ever paying attention to what Jesus requires. ONLY, has happened and God needs your help to change it.

"If a man love me, he will keep my words." – Jesus in John 14:23

Keeping His words are not "optional". The spirit of "optional" in the church paints a picture of a God who doesn't care if you do this or do that because you're saved by confession not action. The optional god says don't rob God by withholding tithes, don't fornicate, then with the same breath say there is no law to live by. This optional spirit says Jesus broke the Sabbath, but then turns and say Jesus lived sin free. This spirit believes John Nelson Darby, John Scofield and other men more than God. These people live under 2nd Peter 3:15-16:

And account that the longsuffering of our Lord is salvation; even as our beloved brother Paul also according to the wisdom given unto him hath written unto you; As also in all his epistles, speaking in them of these things; in which are some things hard to be understood, which they that are unlearned and unstable wrest, as they do also the other scriptures, unto their own destruction.

These people have used Paul's writing the wrong way and it has led them unto their own destruction and unfortunately the destruction of many others. Satan has created the term "New Testament Christian" stripping them of old testament knowledge, which they need to understand what Paul, Jesus and everyone else is talking about. This spirit has twisted the scriptures to justify a life of disobedience. If you have this spirit, cast it out today!

Don' t be one without understanding. You're powerful, you're amazing and you're full of God! Don't turn back to a life of disobedience! God loves you and you can do this! John 3:16 IS POWERFUL, but it becomes powerless, when understanding is void.

Love you and see you in the next chapter...

Behold the LAMB OF GOD

*I*n this chapter I would like to briefly discuss the who, what and why's of Jesus Christ. In John 1:29-30 John calls Jesus "The Lamb of God." He says:

The next day John seeth Jesus coming unto him, and saith, Behold the Lamb of God, which taketh away the sin of the world. This is he of whom I said, After me cometh a man which is preferred before me: for he was before me.

Jesus came here to become The Lamb of God and the job of the lamb was to cleanse the world of its sins by its blood. John also acknowledges that Christ was here before Him, even though John was the older cousin. Jesus was Yahweh (The Son) in the first 39 books of the bible. He was the only one who dealt with Israel as Jesus says "no one has seen nor heard from the Father at any time." That's why Christ's real name is Yahshua, because it means Yahweh has come to bring salvation and that is exactly what Jesus came to do, and did! Through His blood, the most powerful entity to ever exist upon this earth, everyone had and has the opportunity to have their prior acts of lawlessness wiped away.

The question becomes, why?

Why was wiping our sins away needed, so much to the point that Christ had to come in the form of man to save the man that He had created? We've mostly touched on it in the chapter Understanding Grace, however we'll briefly touch it here as well. Christ came because sin equals death! It did then and it does now. But now if you sin, you can call the bails bondsmen, which is The Lord as His blood bails you out, giving you eternal life, instead of a life sentence of damnation. Everybody in Israel knew this and therefore everyone in Israel waited upon The Lamb, which was prophesied to come. Even Simon the man full of the Holy Spirit in Luke 2 said, "Now let me go in peace" because he saw The Lamb that was to be slain. Everybody anticipated His coming. Once Andrew heard John utter that Jesus was the Lamb of God in John 1, the scripture says that he got his brother Peter in John 1:41 and said this:

We have found the Messiah, which is, being interpreted, the Christ.

John didn't say He was The Christ. All this fuss was because John said "Behold, the Lamb of GOD!" Those 5 words had great meaning to those with knowledge. They knew that once Adam sinned in the beginning three types of deaths occurred:

1) The death of man. God told Adam that the day you eat of the

tree you will die! Peter lets us know that a 1000 years to God is liken unto 1 day. Once Adam sinned, man was sentenced to 1000 years of life, and that was it. Methuselah came closest with 969 years of age.

2) The second death was that of an animal. The bible says clothes of animal skin was made by God and given to Adam and Eve. The skin of an animal meant that animal must have died. Blood was shed. God foreshadowed a system that He didn't implement unto 430 years after the promise made to Abraham called The Law of Animal Sacrifice, which foreshadowed the need for Christ's blood to be shed.

3) The most important death that occurred was The Lambs! Revelations 13:8 says, "Christ was the Lamb that was slain at the foundation (beginning) of this world."

The moment Adam sinned, death reigned, and if God wanted to save us, Christ had to come and die the death...HIMSELF! Because of this, everybody waited upon the Messiah, the Lamb, the one who was slain from the foundation of this world, JESUS The Lord and savior of the world.

However, why Christ came seems to be a mystery to many.

What did He change?

What did He replace?

What did He nail to the cross?

For this understanding, we must understand what The Lamb represents. The Lamb represents a covenant that was made between God and Israel. Most people mistakenly look at the first 39 books of the bible and think ITS ALL AN OLD, DONE AWAY WITH COVENANT, which is translated to Testament, and that's not true. Is the Noahtic Covenant, done away with? The one where God shows the rainbow in the sky to let us know He won't flood the earth? No, I just saw a rainbow the other day. What about the Abrahamic Covenant; is there a new covenant for that? Are we not the seeds of Abraham and declare his blessings? Of course we do, so that's not done away with. Well then, what is the OLD COVENANT? Lets take a look at Hebrews 9 as it details the events of the Old Testament we constantly speak of.

Hebrews 9

[1]Then verily the first covenant had also ordinances of divine service, and a worldly sanctuary.[2]For there was a tabernacle made; the first, wherein was the candlestick, and the table, and the shewbread; which is called the sanctuary.[3]And after the second veil, the tabernacle which is called the Holiest of all;[4]Which had the golden censer, and the ark of the covenant [7]But into the second went the high priest alone once every

year, not without blood, which he offered for himself, and for the errors of the people:

[10]Which stood only in meats and drinks, and divers washings, and carnal ordinances, imposed on them until the time of reformation.

[13]For if the blood of bulls and of goats, and the ashes of an heifer sprinkling the unclean, sanctifieth to the purifying of the flesh:

As I skipped around chapter 9, three things of this OLD done away with covenant are very important.

1. A tabernacle had to be built with a veil to get to the Holy of Holies
2. A High Priest had to be set up
3. An animal's blood had to be shed

If the new covenant has replaced this old one, claiming it has a better way, then Christ must have set up a better system through His death and resurrection. Lets see if this happened.

1. The tabernacle and the way to get to the mercy seat of God must be more efficient.

Hebrews 10:19-20:

Having therefore, brethren, boldness to enter into the holiest by the blood of Jesus, by a new and living way, which he hath consecrated for us, through the veil, that is to say, his flesh.

His flesh has become the veil. That's why we pray in the Name of Jesus...His body is pure, perfect, and sin free...not ours. Mark 15:38 says, "And the veil of the temple was rent in twain from the top to the bottom." As soon as Christ died the veil was ripped, letting you know that the veil was no longer needed to gain access to Christ. Thus, a new temple has arose as well. Paul speaks about this new temple in 1 Corinthians 3:16. "Know ye not that ye are the temple of God, and that the Spirit of God dwelleth in you?" You are now the temple and Christ now gives us complete access to the Father through these two arenas. That's new and improved!

What about the second main point of the covenant?

    2. A High Priest had to be set up.

Let's look at Hebrews 7:

[15]And it is yet far more evident: for that after the similitude of Melchisedec there ariseth another priest [21](For those priests were made without an oath; but this with an oath by him that said unto him, The Lord sware and will not repent, Thou art a priest for ever after the order of Melchisedec:) [22]By so much was Jesus made a surety of a better testament. [23]And they truly were many priests, because they were not

suffered to continue by reason of death: [24]But this man, because he continueth ever, hath an unchangeable priesthood. [25]Wherefore he is able also to save them to the uttermost that come unto God by him, seeing he ever liveth to make intercession for them.

So, we plainly see that Christ changed the priesthood from the children of Levi to Himself. Creating a new testament or covenant or law for those that believe in Him; the Law of Faith! The Levi was a sinner just like us, so what good was he to intercede? We needed a non-blemished Lamb. Someone who was sin free and who had all of The Father's attention and that person is Christ. That's a new and improved system.

Thirdly, He must have replaced the need for animal blood. Remember the third major aspect of The Law of Animal Sacrifice?

3. Animal's blood had to be shed.

Let's read about the better way.

Hebrews 10

[1]For the law having a shadow of good things to come, and not the very image of the things, can never with those sacrifices which they offered year by year continually make the comers thereunto perfect. [2]For then would they not have ceased to be

offered? because that the worshippers once purged should have had no more conscience of sins.[3]But in those sacrifices there is a remembrance again made of sins every year. [4]For it is not possible that the blood of bulls and of goats should take away sins. [16]This is the covenant that I will make with them after those days, saith the Lord, I will put my laws into their hearts, and in their minds will I write them; [17]And their sins and iniquities will I remember no more. [18]Now where remission of these is, there is no more offering for sin. [19]Having therefore, brethren, boldness to enter into the holiest by the blood of Jesus.

Here we see that animal blood couldn't remit, or take away sins, but the Blood of JESUS could!

1 Corinthians 5:7-8:

> For even <u>Christ our passover is sacrificed for us</u>: Therefore *let us keep the feast*, not with old leaven, neither with the leaven of malice and wickedness; but with the unleavened bread of sincerity and truth.

Here we see the covenant of animal sacrifice had to be made new and the law that went with it because Christ is our Passover Lamb. There were dozens of commandments attached to The Law of Animal Sacrifice that has been completely done and away with. So now when we sin, we go to HIM, the eternal Lamb of God. This is the Good News. We now have a new priest, new blood and a new way to get to the Father! No more do we have to deal with a sinful man to bring us to God. We HAVE ACCESS TO GOD ourselves! WE CAN BE CLEANSED FROM OUR SINS! WE CAN WALK in Oneness with OUR GOD! WE have an INTERCESSOR that KNOWS OUR STRUGGLES...HE OVERCAME, now WE CAN OVERCOME! They knew that ETERNAL LIFE WAS BACK ON THE TABLE and anyone who served God through His Son, will be SAVED! That's some really good news for those with knowledge!

Hebrews 10:5-10 explains:

> Wherefore when he cometh into the world, he saith, Sacrifice and offering thou wouldest not, but a body hast thou prepared me: In burnt offerings and sacrifices for sin thou hast had no pleasure. Then said I, Lo, I come (in the volume of the book it is written of me,) to do thy will, O God. Above when he said, Sacrifice and offering and burnt offerings and offering for sin thou wouldest not, neither hadst pleasure therein; which are offered by the law; Then said he, Lo, I come to do thy will, O God. He taketh away the first, that he may establish the second.

Here it says that because animal sacrifice wasn't good enough meaning it could only cover sins temporarily. That temporal blood is why, according to Exodus 29:38, God says they had to slay The Lamb daily! And because it wasn't good enough, an ETERNAL sacrifice, had to come. Therefore Christ said, PREPARE ME MARY! I WILL COME THROUGH HER TO SAVE THE MAN THAT I'VE CREATED! Man, that's a love story! And because of that love story, a new, better covenant came with the death and resurrection of The Messiah. The good news isn't that you have nothing else to do. Beware when you hear people say that every law is gone. For we just learned in the previous chapter that Jesus says that NOT ONE JOT OR TITTLE from His royal law shall pass until HEAVEN AND EARTH PASS! Therefore lets continue to study line upon line precept upon precept so that we may gain understanding and access into His Kingdom through the Lamb of God, which is Christ. Now that we're under the blood of power, dominion and authority, let's live like it by submitting our power, dominion and authority over to Him, The Lamb of God.

See you in the next chapter...

Would you still say YES?

My favorite gospel song to date is 'Say Yes' by Shekinah Glory. The singer takes the position of God and asks, "If I told you what I really required of you, would you still say yes?" I mean, really think about it for a second. What if God wanted more from you? What if He said, "Yeah I see everything you're doing, but there's more!" This is how Christ viewed the believers in at the church of Ephesus, Smyrna, Pergamos, Thyatira, Sardis, and the church of the Laodiceans. Maybe, just maybe, God wants more from you too.

If He does, would you really be willing to do it? Would you be willing to drink from the cup of Hosea whom God asked to marry a prostitute or Ezekiel whom God asked to lay on his side for numerous days or Jesus who had to lay down His life for His fellow man? None of these things were punishments nor acts of religion. Every act that God instructs us to do is to be done for one reason and one reason only: because He asked. The God that has loved you is asking you to go to that next level for Him. Think about it, how many times have you asked God for more? Well today, it's His turn.

There are three main misnomers in the Christian church that the Lord wants to correct. There are actually several, but these are three subjects that God wanted me to personally address with you.

1. His Sabbath Still Remains.

I know, your like I was..."WHAT? What does that even mean? Jesus did away with the Sabbath!" Even though we can't read that anywhere in the bible, we're taught The Sabbath no longer exists like it's 90 going north. One of the main reasons this is taught is because many church leaders say that Jesus broke The Sabbath, and if Jesus broke The Sabbath, then it's over. The only problem with that theory is this; JESUS DIDN'T BREAK THE SABBATH. (lol)

Jesus was the <u>unblemished</u> Lamb, meaning that He lived sin free. If you've followed the previous chapters then you know that sin is breaking of a law according to 1st John 3:4. The Sabbath is commandment #4 in the Royal Law. If He broke it, He is not the Messiah because The Messiah couldn't sin. In the book of John after being accused and bashed publically, Jesus confronts the leaders and says, "Can any of you prove me guilty of sin?" And no one could. He also says in John 14 that satan has come and has found nothing in Him.

Jesus did provide further understanding concerning His Sabbath, but not once did He do away with it. Jesus getting rid of the Sabbath would go directly against His words in Matthew 5:17, where Jesus says, "Think not that I've come to destroy the law". Which law is He speaking of? Well immediately Christ starts talking about items found in the Royal Law such as adultery and murder and other statutes that are attached to it as I stated before. This is the same law that The Sabbath comes from. Furthermore, Jesus says this of the same law in the 19th verse of the same chapter, "For verily I say unto you, Till heaven and earth pass, one jot or one tittle shall in no wise pass from the law, till all be fulfilled." Is earth still here? Well then, so is every aspect of that law, which includes The Sabbath.

Another point that's imperative we understand, is that in Genesis 2, it was JESUS who created, therefore it was it was JESUS who set apart the 7th day and it was JESUS who made it holy. John 1:3 lets us know that all things were made by Jesus and without Him was NOTHING made. So with that understanding, is it the Jews Sabbath day, or Jesus'? Let's take a look at Genesis 2:3, it says:

And God blessed the 7th day and sanctified it.

Who did this, the JEW? The Israelite Nation? Nope, the scriptures say, the God we serve did. Jesus set apart the 7th day. Not the 1st, the 2nd or the 3rd day. Jesus decided to set this day apart for a specific reason and today I'm going to show you why.

In Leviticus the 23rd chapter, the weekly Sabbath day pops up when God is teaching the people about His feasts. The word feast means, APPOINTED TIMES. The Sabbath is an APPOINTED TIME, and any specific time that is appointed can only be changed by the one who appointed it, JESUS, not the pope, JESUS, not Constantine the emperor, JESUS, not your pastor, JESUS, and Jesus never changed it. Why wouldn't Jesus change it? Here's why; The seventh day represents the 7000th year. During this 7000th year, man will enter into a rest with God, entitled the New Millennial Period aka 1000 years of rest. Are we in His rest now? NO. Satan is still here. We won't enter into the rest of Christ until satan is locked up for 1000 years according to Revelations 20:2. Paul lets you know that this rest is <u>still to come</u> in Hebrews the 4th chapter.

Hebrews 4

> [1]Let us therefore fear, lest, a promise being left us of entering into his rest, any of you should seem to come short of it. [6]Seeing therefore it remaineth that some must enter therein [9]There remaineth therefore a rest to the people of God. [11]Let us labour therefore to enter into that rest.

I never understood why it's preached that we are in His rest now when Paul clearly states that His rest is still to come. Paul also says in the 4th verse of the same chapter:

> [4]For he spake in a certain place of the seventh day on this wise,
> And God did rest the seventh day from all his works.

Paul is letting us know that the 7th day in Genesis, was merely a foreshadowing to the DAY of rest that is to come. Peter tells us that one day with the Lord is as a 1000 years and a 1000 years is as one day (2nd Peter 3:8). Therefore this 1-day of rest, represents the 1000 years of rest that is to come. But how do you make it in to this 1st Resurrection aka the 1000 years of rest?

Hebrews 4:3:

> For we which have believed do enter into rest.

Remember from the above chapter that the belief Paul is speaking of here is obedience. Remember Paul also says in verse 6 that the Israelites didn't enter in because of UNBELIEF and we read in Joshua and Jeremiah that their unbelief meant that did not OBEY. So those that obey will enter in! Pay attention to one of the points that Paul tells us to make sure we obey as we continue to read.

Hebrew 4:9-11:

> There remaineth therefore a rest to the people of God. For he that is entered into his rest, he also hath ceased from his own works, as God did from his. Let us labour therefore to enter into that rest, lest any man fall after the same example of unbelief.

Paul says there remains a REST. That word REST in Hebrews 4:9 means *sabbatismos (strong's G4520)*.

Therefore Paul is saying there remains a Sabbath for the people of God. Then Paul says that if you want to enter into this 1000 year Sabbath that he's speaking of in verse 9, you must also CEASE from your own works...but how? "AS GOD DID FROM HIS!"

How did God cease from His own works?

On the 7th day, The Sabbath. Don't believe Genesis, well also look at Exodus when He poured manna down from heaven. What day wouldn't He pour? The seventh day! And by the way, this was all done before the 10 commandments of stone were created.

Jesus said in Exodus 31:13:

"Verily my sabbaths ye shall keep: for it is a sign between me and you throughout your generations; that ye may know that I am the LORD that doth sanctify you."

This is Jesus speaking! Here we see Jesus speaking to the Israelites, but did you know that once you become saved you become spiritual Israel as well, engrafted in? Earlier we've learned that every covenant, every promise is to Israel and that now includes you according to Paul in Romans 2:29. But even if you can't wrap your mind around that, God makes sure you understand what He requires of everyman that joins His house.

Isaiah 56:2-6:

Blessed is the man that doeth this, and the son of man that layeth hold on it; that keepeth the sabbath from polluting it, and keepeth his hand from doing any evil. Neither let the son of the stranger, that hath joined himself to the LORD, speak, saying, The LORD hath utterly separated me from his people:

neither let the eunuch say, Behold, I am a dry tree. For thus saith the LORD unto the eunuchs that keep my sabbaths, and choose the things that please me, and take hold of my covenant; even unto them will I give in mine house and within my walls a place and a name better than of sons and of daughters: I will give them an everlasting name, that shall not be cut off. Also the sons of the stranger, that join themselves to the LORD, to serve him, and to love the name of the LORD, to be his servants, every one that keepeth the sabbath from polluting it, and taketh hold of my covenant.

Here Jesus lets you know that EVERYONE that joins Himself to the New Covenant (Gentile etc.) must keep HIS Sabbath. Then in verse 7 it says, that HIS house, will NOW be called the house of prayer for ALL people. So Jesus pictured all His people honoring HIS Sabbath, HIS way. Is it just for the Jew? You've just read that it is for the Jew and EVERYONE ELSE that wants to please HIM.

Did you know that Jesus prophesied through the mouth of Daniel that His Sabbath would be changed in Daniel 7? It says that the 4th Nation to rule the earth, Rome, will change times and laws. The change of the Sabbath went from the 7th day to the 1st day by none other than Constantine, the ROMAN emperor. He changed it, which was wrong, but at least even Constantine, some 300 years after the resurrection of Christ, knew a Sabbath had to be kept.

"Can't we worship everyday?"

Of course we can! Not only can you worship everyday, but many of the believers are documented with reading and praying and worshiping multiple times a day. However, THEY KEPT THE SABBATH, because God asked them too. As we've learned, The Sabbath is about much more than worship, it's about rest along with drawing attention to the rest that is to come. There has been a severe fallen away of knowledge, but now because we're entering into the last days, knowledge shall be increased.

You want to know what else God also says in Daniel 7? That He wants His saints to destroy that kingdom. Of course you can't destroy Rome, Rome isn't bad, but you can destroy the false doctrine that comes from it as I am doing now. Thus leading me to another time-change out of Rome and this is the 2ⁿᵈ thing that God wants you to know.

2. The timing of the Rapture is WRONG!

In 400 A.D. Augustine, a ROMAN, created the IDEA that the church would rapture off, taken away in the twinkling of an eye. And though this is true, for the first time in history, he publicized that this 'Rapture' would take place BEFORE THE TRIBULATION.

Now, I wish this were true, but according to the scriptures it's not. Will God protect His people during this time? YES, only if you follow His instructions. However He lets you know in Revelations that many of His strong saints will get beheaded for His name sake. The timing of the rapture is very important and this is why:

If your pastor is telling you, THE CHURCH WILL BE GONE, you'll never even know a tribulation is going on. You will only see it as global warming and bad government, "The Mark" or chip, that's just the way of the future, that's it! You will jump in line to take the mark of the beast without even thinking twice. You'll see your pastor and the other men and women of God and say, "Well, they're still here. This little mark on my hand or forehead can't be the mark of the beast. The church isn't raptured off yet!" According to the book of Revelations, if you receive the mark, you WILL DRINK THE WINE OF THE WRATH OF GOD! Basically, you're going to the lake of fire...yeah, it's that serious.

Read closely. The basis for Augustine's theory is from I Thessalonians 4:13-17:

> But I would not have you to be ignorant, brethren, concerning them which are asleep, that ye sorrow not, even as others which have no hope. For if we believe that Jesus died and rose again, even so them also which sleep in Jesus will God bring with him. For this we say unto you by the word of the Lord, that we which are alive and remain unto the coming of the Lord shall not prevent (proceed) them which are asleep. For the Lord himself shall descend from heaven with a shout, with the voice of the archangel, and with the trump of God: and the dead in Christ shall rise first: Then we which are alive and remain shall be caught up together with them in the clouds, to meet the Lord in the air: and so shall we ever be with the Lord.

Paul didn't want us to be ignorant concerning the dead. He says that those whom believe, which we know are those that obey, God will bring with HIM. Here's the order of events.

1. The Lord shall descend. And when He does an archangel will blow the trumpet of God.
2. The dead will rise first.
3. Those which are alive shall be "caught up" which is where we get the word 'RAPTURE' from.

Now Paul reiterates this same story in 1 Corinthians 15:51-52:

Behold, I shew you a mystery; We shall not all sleep, but we shall all be changed, in a moment, in the twinkling of an eye, at the last trump: for the trumpet shall sound, and the dead shall be raised incorruptible, and we shall be changed.

Here we see the same order, but now we see THE LAST TRUMP. "In a twinkling of an eye, at the LAST TRUMPET!" Then the dead will be changed (rise first) and those that are alive (we shall be changed.)

But now the question is, WHEN DOES THE LAST TRUMP HAPPEN? Let's Investigate!

Revelations 8:2,6:

²And I saw the seven angels which stood before God; and to them were given seven trumpets. ⁶And the seven angels which

had the seven trumpets prepared themselves to sound.

So there are how many trumpets that will sound? 7. Let's find all 7 trumpets.

Revelations 8:7 - The first angel sounded, and there followed hail and fire mingled with blood, and they were cast upon the earth: and the third part of trees was burnt up, and all green grass was burnt up.

Revelation 8:8 - And the second angel sounded, and as it were a great mountain burning with fire was cast into the sea: and the third part of the sea became blood;

Revelation 8:10 - And the third angel sounded, and there fell a great star from heaven, burning as it were a lamp, and it fell upon the third part of the rivers, and upon the fountains of waters;

Revelation 8:12 - And the fourth angel sounded, and the third part of the sun was smitten, and the third part of the moon, and the third part of the stars; so as the third part of them was darkened, and the day shone not for a third part of it, and the night likewise.

Revelation 9:1 - And the fifth angel sounded, and I saw a star fall from heaven unto the earth: and to him was given the key of the bottomless pit.

Revelation 9:14 - Saying to the <u>sixth</u> angel which had the trumpet, Loose the four angels which are bound in the great river Euphrates.

NOTICE THAT THIS <u>IS</u> THE TRIBULATION! So how can it be said that we will be gone at the first trumpet, when the word of God says the last trumpet? <u>Rome</u> has changed the times again! Lets look at the 7th Trumpet.

Revelation 11:15 - And the <u>seventh</u> angel sounded; and there were great voices in heaven, saying, The kingdoms of this world are become the kingdoms of our Lord, and of his Christ; and he shall reign for ever and ever.

Doesn't this sound like what Paul says would happen in 1st Thessalonians? Of course it does. This also lines up with what <u>JESUS SAYS</u> in Matthew 24. Has anybody read or seen the movies or books that have reached over 100,000,000 people, that starts off with one woman in the field and one is raptured and the other is still here? And one on the rooftop and the other is gone? They get that from the mouth of Jesus, but what JESUS ACTUALLY SAYS is shocking!

Matthew 24:29:

> <u>Immediately after</u> the tribulation of those days shall the sun be darkened, and the moon shall not give her light, and the stars shall fall from heaven, and the powers of the heavens

shall be shaken.

We see that Jesus is talking about what will happen once the tribulation is OVER. Lets skip down to verse 40-41:

> Then shall two be in the field; the one shall be taken, and the other left. Two women shall be grinding at the mill; the one shall be taken, and the other left.

So you mean to tell me, JESUS said that this would happen IMMEDIATELY AFTER the tribulation? Then why have we seen this in the beginning of every movie and read it in the beginning of every book? Satan is a master deceiver, who can know it.

It's up to YOU to spread HIS word, instead of the words and customs of man. If the people do not get this word and accept the mark of the beast because they've been taught a false doctrine, GOD'S heart will continue to grow even more sorrowful than it already has. Simply because the people HE died for, has to be destroyed or thrown into the lake of fire from a lack of knowledge. Please do your part.

3. People WILL be judged for they FOOD they consume!

The last point that God wants to drive home is probably the toughest one of them all. Can you eat whatever you want and make it into the kingdom of heaven? NO! Revelations 2:14 says:

> But I have a few things against thee, because thou hast there them

that hold the doctrine of Balaam, who taught Balac to cast a stumblingblock before the children of Israel, <u>to eat things sacrificed unto idols</u>, and to commit fornication.

So the doctrine of Balaam is what Jesus calls a stumbling block. A stumbling block causes those on a path, to fall. Our path is eternal life and the doctrine of Balaam has caused many of us to stumble as well. Jesus brings up the foods we eat twice, AFTER, his death and resurrection; which falls under the dispensation of grace that we are in now.

But does He really mean literal food

- Does God really care about what we eat?
- Isn't it only what comes out of a man that defiles him?
- Many questions arose during this process and I'm going to walk you through them all.

Now, before we get started, I would like to be the first to tell you that I loved ribs and pork chops, lobsters, shrimp and crab legs all day long, so my feet drug a little on this research, but what I learned slew me and stopped me and changed my life forevermore.

Lets start off with an end time prophecy found in Isaiah 65. I know, I know, Isaiah's the Old Testament right? Yes, but Jesus is speaking through Isaiah about the <u>end times</u> in which WE live in today. All end time prophecy falls under the dispensation of GRACE. With that understanding, let's see what God has to say:

Isaiah 65:1-5:

> I am <u>sought of them that asked not for me</u>; I am found of
> <u>them that sought me not</u>: I said, Behold me, behold me, unto a
> nation that was not called by my name. I have spread out my
> hands all the day unto a rebellious people, which walketh in a
> way that was not good, after their own thoughts; A people that
> provoketh me to anger continually to my face; that sacrificeth
> in gardens, and burneth incense upon altars of brick; Which
> remain among the graves, and lodge in the monuments, which
> eat swine's flesh, and broth of abominable things is in their
> vessels; Which say, Stand by thyself, come not near to me; for I
> am holier than thou. These are a smoke in my nose, a fire that
> burneth all the day.

Many people think God is talking about Israel, but that's not the
case. Israel is documented as calling upon the name of Yahweh since
the beginning of time. The forefathers, such as Abraham and Enoch,
and Jacob's heart was intertwined with God's. During the 400 years
of slavery, God said He heard THEIR cry, so this is most certainly not
Israel. God is referring to Non-Israelite Nations, such as the Gentiles.
The first Gentile to join the church was Cornelius, AFTER Christ had
already risen. This is the NEW TESTAMENT CHURCH being spoken of
here. This is a prophecy for the generations of Grace.

So, with that understanding, these Gentiles ate from a pig and that
act was a smoke in the nostrils of God? That's what Jesus just said.

Lets see what else Jesus said in Isaiah 66:15-18:

> For, behold, the LORD will come with fire, and with his chariots like a whirlwind, to render his anger with fury, and his rebuke with flames of fire. For by fire and by his sword will the LORD plead with all flesh: and the slain of the LORD shall be many. They that sanctify themselves, and purify themselves in the gardens behind one tree in the midst, <u>eating swine's flesh</u>, and the abomination, and the mouse, shall be <u>consumed</u> together, saith the LORD. For I know their works and their thoughts: it shall come, that I will gather all nations and tongues; and they shall come, and see my glory.

This is end time JUDGMENT! Jesus will come with a fire and a sword as re-illustrated in Revelations and Jeremiah. Jesus said He WILL SLAY those that eat the flesh of pigs. THIS INCLUDES THE NEW TESTAMENT CHURCH, Jesus hasn't come back yet!!!! Get this, Jesus didn't just say the nation of Israel, Jesus said He's gathering all the nations to do this. WHICH INCLUDES THE NEW TESTAMENT CHURCH!

So does Jesus care about what you eat?

According to Him, He does.

However, people have misunderstood some passages of scripture that I would love to BRIEFLY address with you today.

Matthew 15 and Mark 7 tell the same story about Jesus eating with unwashed hands. The New NIV writers as well as many other pastors have thought this to be the place in which JESUS CLEANSED

ALL FOODS. It doesn't say that, so the NIV writers <u>IMPLEMENTED</u> "this is where Jesus cleansed all foods" in Mark the 7th Chapter, which was blatant and deceivingly done. No translation from the Greek to the Hebrew to the King James Version even slightly allude to this! It was simply added. Adding to the bible is WRONG! Nevertheless, lets investigate the matter. Let's look at the Matthew 15 version:

> [1]Then came to Jesus Scribes and Pharisees, which were of Jerusalem, saying,[2]Why do thy disciples transgress the tradition of the elders? for they wash not their hands when they eat bread.[11]Not that which goeth into the mouth defileth a man; but that which cometh out of the mouth, this defileth a man. (said Jesus)

Then we're about to see <u>Peter</u> needed some extra understanding of this, which is important.

> [15]Then answered Peter and said unto him, Declare unto us this parable.[16]And Jesus said, Are ye also yet without understanding?[17]Do not ye yet understand, that whatsoever entereth in at the mouth goeth into the belly, and is cast out into the draught?[18]But those things which proceed out of the mouth come forth from the heart; and they defile the man.[19]For out of the heart proceed evil thoughts, murders, adulteries, fornications, thefts, false witness, blasphemies:
>
> [20]These are the things which defile a man: but <u>to eat with unwashen hands defileth not a man</u>.

He told Peter, point blank, this is about eating with dirty hands. This is an important passage because some years later, Peter, in Acts 10, had a vision about eating unclean foods that God sanctified or set-apart in The Book of Leviticus. Peter, the same one whom pulled Jesus to the side in Matthew and Mark for further understanding, had this to say after he heard "slay and eat" unclean foods, "I have never eating anything unclean."

Get this, Peter, the one who got further understanding about what Christ said in Matthew 15 and Mark 7, didn't think he had a license to eat all foods. If he had, Peter would have said, OK, I ALREADY UNDERSTAND WE CAN EAT EVERYTHING, but Peter said "Not so Lord," and then he went away and the scripture said "he doubted the vision." He doubted it, because Peter read what the Prophets said will happen to those that eat unclean foods, the same passages we just read.

Then we see God shows Peter that the vision he had was about Gentiles entering into the church and NOT about food at all! It was ONLY about letting the Gentiles into the church according to PETER. That's what Peter says out of his very own mouth later in Acts. Let me show you. Acts 10:28 Peter says this of the vision:

And he said unto them, Ye know how that it is an unlawful thing for a man that is a Jew to keep company, or come unto one of another nation; but God hath shewed me that I should not call any man common or unclean.

From this point on, the Gentiles and all other nations were able to be part of Gods church. Why have we created something different? Why are we saying that this is about eating food when clearly it's not? God shows visions of symbols such as Jacobs ladder. It didn't mean God wanted Jacob to build a ladder and climb to heaven. It's like the Lord showing you a vision of a car passing as stop sign. God probably isn't talking about you and your driving, however it may be about your need to stop something that is outside the will of God. These are elementary facts of Christianity.

Romans 14, is another place that is misunderstood, simply due to not reading the complete thoughts of Paul. Therefore people have used this to dispel what God said from the mouth of His prophets, but once you read it, you will see it's ONLY talking about vegetarians vs. meat eaters.

I Timothy 4, is another place. Paul is talking to people who "know and believe the truth." What was the measure of truth at that time? The Old Testament! That's why Paul taught the people about Jesus from the OLD TESTAMENT to prove Jesus was the Messiah. And then Paul goes on to say in I Timothy 4, "For every creature of God is good, and nothing to be refused, if it be received with thanksgiving:"

Now if you just stop here, you're right, we can eat anything, but Paul doesn't stop here! Let's continue to read.

I Timothy 4:5:

For it is sanctified by the word of God and prayer.

Paul says the foods I'm speaking of are sanctified or set-apart by The Word of God. Did God set apart foods in the Word of God? YES! He called them clean and unclean foods. It was set apart before a Jew was even created! In Genesis, Jesus instructed Noah to bring clean animals in 7x7 and unclean 2x2. But if you haven't studied the Old Testament, then how would you possibly know this? Latter He gave Moses all the foods that were separated during the times of Noah, in Leviticus 11.

And last but not least, I will bring you to *2ⁿᵈ Colossians*. This is the 2ⁿᵈ most misunderstood chapter in the bible next to John 3, so I will take a little time to break this one down for you.

1ˢᵗ were going to review some of Paul's other writing:

- 1 Timothy 4:12 - <u>Let no man</u> despise thy youth
- 2ⁿᵈ Thessalonians 2:3 - <u>Let no man</u> deceive you by any means
- Titus 2:15 - These things speak, and exhort, and rebuke with all authority. <u>Let no man</u> despise thee

Paul often speaks of this "no man" and each time it's used with a negative connotation. Paul's NO MAN, is a man that is not influenced by God 100% of the time Paul uses it.

So lets see if this example holds true in Colossians 2.

Colossians 2:

⁸Beware lest any man spoil you through philosophy and vain deceit, after the tradition of men, after the rudiments of the

world, and not after Christ.

What type of man would take you away from the traditions of Christ? An ungodly man!

[18]Let no man beguile you of your reward

What type of man would beguile you of your reward? An ungodly man!

Now, with that understanding, lets look at Colossians 2:16:

Let no man therefore judge you in meat, or in drink, or in respect of an holyday, or of the new moon, or of the sabbath days:

Paul is saying, don't let unlearned, unholy people, talk about you or discourage you from God's standard of foods consumed and Sabbath days that all of Paul's followers kept! Why would Paul say this? Because the unlearned man wants you to go to hell with him!

Paul kept the Sabbaths! Acts 14 and 18 lets you know Paul taught the Gentiles, EVERY Sabbath day. 8 different times in Acts it plainly tells you this.

- Drunkards will not make it into the kingdom (Galatians 5:21).
- People who eat certain meats will be cut off (Isaiah 66:17).
- Christians who break the commandments without repenting for them will go to the lake of fire (Revelations 21:27).

The things mentioned in Colossians were never traditions of man, these have ALWAYS been traditions of JESUS. There were and still are, shadows that point to the coming of our Messiah. Our reward comes from the "One who is to come," which is Jesus. Let's read it:

Revelations 22:12-14:

> And, behold, I come quickly; and my reward is with me, to give every man according as his work shall be. I am Alpha and Omega, the beginning and the end, the first and the last. Blessed are they that <u>do his commandments</u>, that they may have right to the tree of life, and may enter in through the gates into the city.

Your reward is eternal life. Doing the things God tells us to, are liken unto a shadow of what's to come. Like you going to work is a shadow of your paycheck coming. Honoring God's commandments is essential for eternal life with Christ. No matter how clever you put it, Christ is not physically here now. He says in HIS WORD, that when He comes back to this earth, EVERYONE will know it and HIS FEET will touch the Mount of Olives FIRST in Zechariah 14 and Acts 1!

Unfortunately our pastors have failed us on these things and God wants you to know about it. They fall under the prophecy of Isaiah 56:10-12:

His watchmen are blind: they are all ignorant, they are all

dumb dogs, they cannot bark; sleeping, lying down, loving to slumber. Yea, they are greedy dogs which can never have enough, and they are shepherds that cannot understand: they all look to their own way, every one for his gain, from his quarter. Come ye, say they, I will fetch wine, and we will fill ourselves with strong drink; and to morrow shall be as this day, and much more abundant.

And thus, this chapter was created. The reason God wanted to bring this to your attention is so you can REPENT for these things. Some churches teach you that repenting for breaking the Sabbath or eating unclean foods is foolish, but as we've read via the prophets, its foolish not to. Even Jesus tells His disciples "O fools, and slow of heart to believe all that the prophets have spoken." Don't be a fool, love God back with all your heart, mind, and soul.

God wanted you to know, because it is IMPOSSIBLE to repent or turn from something that you DON'T KNOW IS WRONG. You can't turn from something you know nothing about. Repent and die daily.

In God's Timing,

Erik K. Nance for The University of Believers

CPSIA information can be obtained at www.ICGtesting.com
Printed in the USA
LVOW040357091112

306562LV00003B/48/P